District Nurse

Born in Belfast in July 1922, Patricia left her home town in 1944 to embark on a nursing career, beginning at Clare Hall Sanatorium, Barnet, before going to train at the North Middlesex Hospital, where she gained her S. R. N. Certificate in 1948. After a short period there as a Staff Nurse, she returned to Belfast to work for a year at Musgrove Park Hospital. She left for England once more to study at Sharoe Green Hospital, Preston, where she received her State Certified Midwifery Certificate in 1951, and in 1961 she was awarded the National Certificate of District Nursing.

District Nurse

PATRICIA JORDAN

An Orion paperback

First published in Great Britain in 1977
by Weidenfeld & Nicolson
This paperback edition published in 2012
by Orion Books Ltd,
Orion House, 5 Upper St Martin's Lane,
London WC2H 9EA

An Hachette UK company

3 5 7 9 10 8 6 4

A CIP catalogue record for this book
is available from the British Library.

ISBN 978-1-4091-3870-9

Typeset at the Spartan Press Ltd,
Lymington, Hants

Printed and bound in Great Britain by Clays Ltd, St Ives plc

The Orion Publishing Group's policy is to use papers that
are natural, renewable and recyclable products and
made from wood grown in sustainable forests. The logging
and manufacturing processes are expected to conform to
the environmental regulations of the country of origin.

www.orionbooks.co.uk

To Leigh 'Reggie' Crutchley,
for his confidence and encouragement

Chapter One

As I knocked, a piece of flaking paint fell from the door, a dog yelped, and a woman's voice screamed, 'Come round to the bloomin' back, and shut yer bloomin' gob, will yer.' Since I hadn't spoken I wasn't sure whether either remark was directed at me. I knocked again. The voice, nearer this time, said, 'Ruddy deaf are yer, I told yer, come round the bloomin' back.' With my heavy delivery bag in my left hand and the black leather case containing the gas and air apparatus tucked under my left arm, I opened the latch of a side gate with a frozen finger, took an uncertain pace into the dark alley ahead of me, missed a step, and stumbled into a bicycle which fell to the ground with me and my equipment on top of it.

Not a very good beginning to my first assignment as a relief district midwife. There had been enough swearing in a short space of time, so I bit my tongue as I rubbed my shins through torn stockings. I tried remembering that the patient's needs must remain uppermost in my mind. I picked up the bicycle, put it against the wall, grabbed my bag and case and resumed my inky journey.

As I approached what I thought must be the back door, it swung open and from a shaft of light the same raucous voice called, 'Charlie won't be goin' ter t'whippets tonight. 'e's doin' a 'alf turn'; then the door slammed.

I began to think I'd been given the wrong address; by the way this woman spoke she didn't sound as if she was in labour, and surely Charlie, whom I presumed was her husband, wouldn't be doing an extra half shift at work if she was. At least she would be able to tell me where Mrs Caine, my patient, lived, so very gingerly I knocked with my knuckles on the door. A sharp-faced, dark-haired woman of about thirty-five, but looking older, opened it.

'Ah told yer . . .' she began, then peering at me said, 'Oh it's you – the nurse – well, don't just stand there, come in, it's ruddy cold.'

'Mrs Caine?' I queried.

'Ah'm not Mrs Caine, my name's Farmer – Alma Farmer. There's no Mrs Caine in this 'ouse. It's our Pearl you want. She's in t'parlour.' She crooked her thumb over her shoulder and sniffed, 'Mrs bloomin' Caine indeed. She's a ruddy tart, that's what she is, and what my Charlie's goin' to say when 'e gets 'ome and finds 'er 'ere I dread to think. 'e can be very awkward can my Charlie. 'e made me swear last time never to let 'er in again. This'll be the third time she's laid down in this 'ouse, and 'e ain't goin' to like it one little bit, so you'd better look out.'

'Who is Pearl then?' my voice quavered.

'Me bloomin' sister, worse luck, she's me flesh and blood, so I can't turn 'er away, can I?'

I didn't think it much good her looking to me for support, still it cost me nothing to give it at the moment, so I nodded in agreement.

'Well, 'adn't you better go in and see Pearl then?' she said aggrievedly, as if ashamed at having asked my opinion. 'You'll find 'er on t' sofa.'

'Isn't there a bed . . .' I began.

'What! Our Charlie would go bloomin' mad if she 'ad it in ours, and she ain't usin' the kids' room. 'ell, I'd forgotten them.' She opened the door. ''Azel, where yer at?' she shouted.

''Ere, our mam,' a voice replied.

'Where's our Mark? If you've let 'im play in that ruddy water again, I'll kill yer. Get yerself in 'ere and bring 'im with yer.'

I felt it was time to make myself scarce, so I picked up my equipment and went into the parlour. I took a quick glance round. It was, I thought, a squalid little room, though I've seen worse since. The floor was covered in chipped brown lino, there was a piano against one of the walls, the only table was piled with papers and magazines, the tattered, grimy curtains were held together with a clothes peg, there were two rexine chairs, and a matching two-seater sofa; this had been drawn up in front of a coal fire. On the sofa, from where I was standing, I could see a dank head of hair lolling on one side, a skinny arm was thrown over the back, two knees were sticking out over the other side and in the middle protruded a very pregnant abdomen. Groans and muttered curses came from this unattractive form.

'Good evening,' I said. 'I'm the district midwife.'

She half turned her head, 'What's so muckin' good about it? Ah've not known many worse. Come on in then, and shut the bloomin' door after yer, there's a draught.'

I walked to the other side of the sofa to get a proper look at her. She was lying on a grubby sheet, under which was an old dirty mackintosh. Although she was streaming with sweat, as much from the heat of the fire as from the labour pains and, despite the fact that she no longer had any makeup on, she was attractive in a savage sort of way. 'Ah'm Pearl,' she announced sullenly, more to her bulging belly than to me. Suddenly the whole situation struck me as ludicrous. No name could have been less fitting under the circumstances and in the surroundings. The tune 'What Girls Do for Pearls' started strumming in my head. I pulled myself to my five-foot-two height. 'It's what you've got to do for Pearl that matters now,' I thought.

I looked around for somewhere to put my nursing bag, my coat and the gas and air equipment. 'Never leave these things on an unclean surface,' I'd been taught in my midwifery training. 'If circumstances in the home prevent the use of a sheet or a towel, newspapers can be used.' But dare I ask Alma for any of these things?

I put my nursing bag on top of the piano, and alongside

it I stood the gas and air machine. I folded my coat and lay it on one of the armchairs; it was later that I discovered it was covered in dog's hairs. As I moved to examine Pearl, Alma came into the room. ''Ow's she doin'? Is she gonna be long? My Charlie'll be back soon. It should be easy enough, she's 'ad two others. I ask yer, nurse, fancy making the same mistake three times. She must be soft in t''ead.'

'Buzz off,' came the reply, from the form on the sofa.

'Charmin' ain't she, and grateful after me givin' 'er shelter, tellin' me that, in me own 'ouse.'

I saw no point in getting involved, so I began my examination and asked Pearl to stretch her legs out so that I could have a proper look at her tummy. It sounded a bit incongruous to call it that, but it was the way obstetricians and midwives had referred to it during my training.

As I helped Pearl stretch herself out I thought of that training, of the conditions under which I learned to deliver babies, and of the other tummies I'd seen in the past. They had varied greatly in size, and had always been poised on couches in ante-natal clinics, in spotlessly clean and well-equipped surroundings. On the left of each couch had stood a table or glass trolley, on which were laid out a sphygmomanometer (for measuring blood pressure), a stethoscope, foetal stethoscope, rubber gloves, obstetrical cream, and a variety of kidney-shaped dishes. On the floor there had been an enamel pail to receive the used gloves. The snow-white covers of the couch were always changed between examinations.

Then later, I had seen these tummies in the labour ward, pointing towards the ceiling from the hard firm surface of the labour bed. I had learnt to treat them with deference. I'd patted them affectionately and cuddled them close to my ear as I counted the foetal heartbeats, which I checked at regular and increasing intervals as labour progressed. By the time these tummies had reached the labour ward they were hard and rigid through the hefty contractions of the muscular and highly vascular uteruses underneath. They moved spasmodically, sometimes in strong, jumpy jerks as the foetuses struggled gallantly to escape from their humid surroundings into the light.

Within easy reach of the bed, yet far enough away for it not to be contaminated by even the slightest touch of anything that was not aseptic, was a double-shelved glass trolley, draped with a green sterile towel. Under this towel were stainless steel bowls, more kidney-shaped dishes, two small ointment pots, ligatures to tie the umbilical cord, two Spencer Wells clamps and specially blunted umbilical scissors. On the bottom shelf were a sterile syringe and needles, an ampoule of Ergometrine (a drug given after delivery to stimulate the contractions of the uterus and so, it was hoped, prevent a post partum haemorrhage), a bottle of Savlon, another of sterile water and finally two identity bracelets to attach to the left leg and arm of the new baby. When the baby's arrival was imminent, the midwife in charge (we called her the 'scrubbed nurse') would remove the drape from the trolley, while an unscrubbed nurse, without touching the trolley, would fill one of the large bowls with Savlon and one of the ointment pots with sterile water, which were to be used to bathe the baby's eyes.

When the infant arrived, it was held upside down, given the usual smack on the bottom to make it cry, and placed by the 'scrubbed nurse' on a sterile bath towel near at hand. A Spencer Wells clamp was attached to the mother's end of the umbilical cord, another to the baby's end and the cord was cut. This brand new and independent human being was now taken over by the unscrubbed nurse, who extracted any excess mucus from its lungs, and placed it in a cot or an incubator, according to its condition. Meanwhile the 'scrubbed nurse' performed the third stage of labour, and, when the placenta had been completely expelled from the mother, started kneading her tummy like a piece of dough, in this way stimulating the contraction of the womb, until the empty uterus could be felt like a small hard football. Always around had been extra pairs of hands ready to make the mother as comfortable as possible, and a resident doctor was on instant call should any difficulties be experienced.

Alma's 'Well, aren't yer goin' to do summat', and a muttered curse from Pearl, brought me back from my dream world to the stark, wretched reality of a situation I'd not been trained to expect. I found my hands and my knees were trembling. 'I suppose yer know what yer at, I take it you've brought a baby before, 'aven't yer,' Alma half sneered. It was what I needed to goad me into action.

I knelt with my back to the fire at the front of the sofa, and began my examination.

I patted Pearl's tummy, as I'd patted many others. I dug my palms into the flesh to try to find which side the baby was lying in. Despite Pearl's awkward position I was successful – it was on the left. I then groped for the tennisball feel of the foetal head, but it had gone through the brim of Pearl's pelvis; this was good, it was well fixed in position. Cuddling her tummy I placed the foetal stethoscope on the left side of it, and with my watch counted the loud and regular lub-dubs of the tiny heart. All the time I was conscious that Alma's critical eyes were on what I was doing. I also suddenly became aware of a smell of scorching, and of a searing pain in my back. I jumped to my feet. I thought my clothes were alight. 'Feelin' a bit 'ot, eh?' was Alma's unhelpful comment, but she did have the courtesy to help me push the sofa away from the fire.

I knew that a vaginal examination was now necessary, but before I could do it I had to have some hot water and a towel to get as near as I could to being a 'scrubbed nurse'. I plucked up courage and asked Alma for them. She responded and soon reappeared with a large blue polythene bowl which she placed on the seat of the remaining rexine chair, and over the back slung a ragged, but reasonably clean, towel. Stuck to the bottom of the bowl was a piece of red carbolic soap. Things were looking up. I took a scrub brush from my nursing bag and plunged my hands into near boiling water. It was my turn to swear, but resisting the temptation I brusquely asked for some cold water. When this was brought I did as good a job as possible to make my hands and arms aseptic. I slipped on my rubber gloves and moved in to start my examination. I leant over the arm of the sofa; as I touched her, Pearl gave an almighty scream, drew her right knee up, hitting me under the chin and knocking me sideways. This got a chuckle from Alma. 'You wouldn't think she'd got the strength in them skinny legs, would yer?' she leered. When I'd recovered my balance and my courage, I began again. My 'Now, Pearl, it's not really hurting you' was met with a string of obscenities, and by the time the examination was finished I was astonished at how many prefixes can be attached to the word 'off'.

Alma by now had got into the spirit of the thing, and at every expletive from Pearl would jeer, 'Serves yer ruddy right.' Since at last I felt I was commanding some sort of respect, I mentioned that we should be preparing a cot for the baby. 'Yer didn't bring no cot with yer, did yer, Pearl?' said Alma. Since Pearl offered no reply I ventured that possibly we might have the one Alma had used for her children. It was a grave error of judgement. 'What! Use our cot for Pearl's little bastard, not bloomin' likely! My Charlie would 'alf kill me if we did.' This started Pearl off, and the two women went at each other hammer and tongs, with venom and hatred multiplied by expletives. When eventually I was able to get a word in edgeways, I suggested that a laundry basket and pillow would be adequate. I also beseeched Alma, for the child's sake, to find what she could in the way of clothing and nappies. Her face looked set for an obstinate refusal. I played what I thought must be my last card, 'Even baby Jesus had a better birth than this one's likely to get.' It worked. There was a moment of absolute silence, Alma's face changed, she sniffed and left the room, eventually to return with a laundry basket and cushion, two worn baby vests and gowns, and four ragged nappies.

'The best I can do,' she said, as she spread them on the hearth in front of the fire. 'I would 'ave lent 'er the cot only I know Charlie would crucify me,' she almost apologized.

Flushed with my success I now asked for a large pan to boil my bowls and instruments in.

'Gawd, what'll yer want next? I 'aven't got one, but I'll ask around,' she added quickly.

A neighbour must have obliged for she was back with what I needed in ten minutes. I took it to the kitchen, packed the pan with the instruments and bowls, filled it with water, and lit the gas.

My examination had shown that Pearl's cervix was two fingers dilated and that if things went by the book it would be at least an hour or two before I needed the instruments, but I was determined to get things prepared; after all Charlie would be back soon and I might need time to cope with him.

My thought must have fathered his arrival, for at that moment the Burrowdale Town Hall clock struck eight, the back door opened and I heard Charlie, as he went into the living room, call, 'Oo's a bonnie lass then, come and give us a kiss.' This was not what I'd expected to hear when he greeted Alma, and I conveyed my astonishment to Pearl. 'It's not 'er 'e's talkin' to, yer fool, it's 'is ruddy whippet. Thinks more of that bloomin' dog than any 'uman, the ignorant bastard. Baby Doll, 'e calls 'er. You'll 'ear what 'e calls our Alma when 'e discovers I'm 'ere.' I did, for Charlie, moving into the kitchen to find out what was cooking for his dinner, saw my instruments, which I hoped had now come to the boil.

'Alma, what the bloomin' 'ell are these, what's goin' on around 'ere?' he shouted.

To describe the row that followed as Alma attempted to explain things to him would be like reciting a wall of graffiti. By now the whole street must have known what was going on. The gas under my instruments was turned off. 'Ah'm payin' naught in gas bills for that tart,' he cried as he did it, 'and there's no more muckin' coal going into t' parlour.' That didn't worry me, it was already quite hot enough in the house. I could tell by the way Alma shouted back that she was scared out of her wits. I sat on the side of the sofa, holding Pearl's hand – more, I'm ashamed to say, to receive comfort rather than give it. Pearl was the only one who seemed unconcerned, which was astonishing as Charlie kept threatening to come into the parlour and 'sort out yon filth good and proper'.

'Don't worry, nurse, 'e's all talk,' said Pearl, and then

shouted, 'Shurrup yer loud-mouthed swine.' This started a slanging match through the wall.

I could stand it no longer. I rushed into the living room and confronted Charlie: 'Be quiet! Have you no sense of decency or respect? There's a woman in there in pain, I don't care what she is or what she's done, she's suffering and I'm here to help her through it. There's a baby being born, who'll meet evil soon enough. Keep it away from it this night, for God's sake.'

Charlie's big hulk sank into a chair. Baby Doll jumped on to his lap; he stroked her tentatively muttering, 'Oo's a bonnie lass then?' Then he looked at me, 'All right, nurse, we'll shut up, and you can get on with yer job, only don't be too long about it, understand?'

When I rejoined Pearl she looked at me almost with respect, 'That's tellin''im, nurse. You put 'im in 'is place proper, bloomin' bully, that's all 'e is. Now we can get on with t'job.'

It was as if throughout the turmoil Pearl had become immune to pain. She soon made up for lost time, for the contractions became stronger and were occurring at regular intervals of a quarter of an hour. With each recurrent pain she began screaming, drawing up her legs, kicking the arms of the sofa, swearing and blaspheming loudly. I took a syringe from my bag and filled it from an ampoule of pethidine. When she saw what I was at Pearl said, 'And what do yer think yer goin' to do with that thing?' I explained that I was about to inject her with it.

'Not on yer Nelly; yer not stickin' that thing into me.'

'All right,' I soothed her, 'I'll put it down here for the time being,' and I laid it on a towel near the hearth. 'Just turn over on your side for a moment,' I said, and helped her move. I then made a quick grab for the syringe, found the muscle in her bottom, stuck the needle firmly in and was discharging its contents when Pearl flung her arms out and with a 'Yer bloomin' bitch yer' tried to get at the needle. She was too late. 'There you are, it didn't hurt much,' I said as I backed away, just in case she kicked out at me. But things were now happening too fast for her to consider revenge. I looked round for somewhere to put the gas and air machine, for she was nearing the stage when she would be in need of its soothing fumes. I wouldn't have minded a few puffs of it myself!

Since one chair was occupied by the polythene bowl and would also be required for my instruments, I threw my coat on the floor, pulled that chair to the head of the sofa, and opening the case drew the snake-like rubber tube attached to the cylinder from it, bringing it and the face mask over Pearl's right shoulder. She was obviously familiar with this bit of equipment for she made no comment as I did it, and, when I told her that as she felt the next pain in her back she was to take the mask and breathe deeply from it, she replied sullenly, 'I know what to do, it isn't me first, yer know.' I then turned on the mixture of nitrous oxide gas and oxygen.

It was now that I realized I was in danger of breaking

yet another midwife's rule, for when this gas is administered during a home confinement a third person has to be in the room with the patient. Not because of any danger, but to safeguard the nurse, in case she is later accused of stealing something while the patient is in a drowsy state. I decided to get Alma. I tapped on the living-room door. Charlie's 'Come on in' sounded as if he was spoiling for a fight. He was alone, except for Baby Doll, who slipped off his lap and made towards me, sniffing suspiciously.

'Alma's upstairs with t'kids,' he volunteered, before I could ask. 'Anythin' I can do?' I shuddered at the thought.

'No thank you,' I replied. As I stood there, feeling like a spare part, I looked down at the whippet, with its tail between its legs. 'You look like I feel,' I thought, and in sympathy I stooped down to stroke it. The dog seemed to like me, for she put her paws on my shoulder and began licking my cheeks. Charlie's face lit up, 'Ee, that's rare, that's very rare. She don't do that to many. She's taken to you 'as Baby Doll.'

'This is my breakthrough,' I thought, and decided to capitalize on it. I asked how old she was, about her pedigree, whether she'd won any races and pretended a knowledge I didn't have. It didn't matter, Charlie was only too anxious to do the talking. Eventually, when Alma returned, he put his arm round my shoulder and said, 'She's a good 'un, this 'un, understands about dogs, and they understand 'er. So you can get 'er a cup of tea, luv.' I remarked that I must be returning to my patient. 'That

no-good tart, she's rubbish, she's not worth yer trouble,'
he was back to his old self again. I must have looked
concerned. 'Oh I'm not blamin' you for what she's done.'
That, I thought drily, was a comfort. 'All right, you go on
in, and Alma will bring t' tea to yer.'

Cheered by Charlie's change of attitude towards me,
Alma brought a cup for Pearl as well. She helped her sit
up while she drank it. I then asked if she would stay with
me while Pearl was taking the gas. 'No,' she replied, 'I'm
better in there, keepin' 'im 'appy while the goin's good.' I
was sure she was right; together we helped Pearl to lie
down, and then she went. Pearl was now getting very
drowsy and from time to time dropped off to sleep, snor-
ing and swearing alternately. I checked her pulse and the
foetal heartbeat, then leant back against the sofa to rest.
It had been a very exhausting few hours.

My mind went back over my childhood. What would
Sister Benedict, my headmistress, say if she could see
me now? I remembered how, as a fifth former, she had
warned me of the big, bad, wicked world that lay outside
the convent walls, and of the iniquities of the people in
that world. Was my present situation the kind of thing
she was trying to tell me about? How would she, with her
gentleness and naivety, have responded to Pearl, Alma or
Charlie? Come to think of it, when I'd expressed an interest in nursing she'd played down the virtues of Florence
Nightingale. As a Dominican, the order of teachers, she
had rather extolled the merits of that profession, which

was probably why I chose neither at the time, but became a secretary to a stockbroker, a Mr Isaacs, a quiet, likeable, pipe-smoking man, whose bottom I got to know better than his face, for he always spoke or dictated with his back to me. When he reprimanded me with his 'Vot have I done to deserve this?', it was from the same position, and when I told him of my decision to leave to follow nursing as a career, his 'Vi you do this to me?' came from over his shoulder. 'Yes, Mr Isaacs,' I now thought, 'Vot have I done to deserve this?' and 'Vi should I do this to myself?'

Then I thought of my home and my parents. It was, I suppose, a home of love, but it was the love of God that predominated, and the affection of my parents was given almost grudgingly, as if in fear that it might be allied with sin. I remembered one evening, I must have been nineteen at the time, I was filling the teapot and accidentally poured boiling water on my feet and blamed 'the bloody kettle'. My mother's face paled, she crossed herself and ordered me to confession immediately. When she reported the incident to my father, he spoke of getting a bishop to the house because a member of his family had used 'some terrible bad talk'. My thoughts returned to my present surroundings. This place, it seemed, would need a platoon of popes to edify it.

Then I thought of the reason for my sudden decision to become a nurse. It had been no vocational calling, but had been caused by a dark-haired, sullenly handsome, Irish boy, Paul Mulholland, storming out of our tennis

club one evening, vowing never to see me again. The
Irish troubles had started for me many years before they
became everyday news. Paul, like myself, was a Catholic;
we became friendly as children, cycling to school together.
Our affection for each other had grown over the years,
and it was assumed by everyone who knew us that we
would eventually get married. There was one shadow that
occasionally fell between us: he was a staunch Republican;
his father, who died when he was young, had been in
prison as a political prisoner during the 1916 rebellion. I,
on the other hand, hated violence. One day a policeman, a
neighbour of ours, was shot and killed, leaving a wife and
six children. Paul was triumphant about this, called the
gunman a hero, and when I protested he sneered at me.
A row began in which things were said that could never
be taken back, and although I felt my cause was just, my
sense of bereavement when he walked out was as great as
the constable's widow's. There seemed no alternative but
for me to leave Belfast, and Ireland, and start a new life.
'I suppose, Paul, if you could see me now,' I thought, 'you
would say it serves me right.'

An oath from Pearl brought me back to reality. She
was wriggling and grunting her way to the edge of the
sofa. I went over and saw that the sheet on which she
was lying was soaked with amniotic fluid, so I knew that
the membranes of the sac in which she was carrying her
baby had now ruptured. Once again I scrubbed my hands
and arms in the basin, slipped on my rubber gloves and

began a further examination. This showed that the cervix, the neck of the womb, had been completely taken up and was fully dilated. I traced the sutures, the soft, fibrous tissue which separates the bones of the foetal skull, with the forefinger of my right hand, while Pearl continued to grunt and swear.

Now, Paul, my parents and the convent nuns were forgotten, and so were the second thoughts I'd had on my choice of career. This was my life's purpose – Pearl and her baby needed me. So what if the conditions were appalling? Didn't that make it more of a challenge?

I was in a kind of ecstasy. I bounded out of the room and kicked open the living-room door, 'Charlie, get the fire made up, and put the kettle on the stove; and hurry. Alma, clean sheets please, then come and hold Pearl's right leg high out of my way.' They moved, and moved fast, without questioning. They seemed to catch the urgency of my mood. I took the pan containing my instruments from the gas, drained it and returned to the parlour. I put on a mask and the shapeless delivery gown, knelt on the floor, and with Alma holding Pearl's leg in the air, got hold of the soft slippery crown of the baby's head with my right hand, but at the end of the last big contraction it slipped back.

'Gawd, bloomin' hurry will yer. I can't stand much more,' Pearl cried.

'Don't speak to me like that,' I shouted back at her.

The whole house seemed to take on a stillness. Charlie,

back in the living room, must have taken my remark personally, for the silence was broken by an almost embarrassed 'Oo's a bonnie lass then?' as if he was seeking comfort from his whippet.

So a baby boy was born, in a peace which had seemed impossible a couple of hours ago. Even Pearl seemed to sense the occasion, for she recovered without swearing, and then asked the usual questions that the mothers in aseptic labour wards put to me – 'What is it? Is he all right?' and the inevitable 'How much does he weigh?' as if all new babies arrived with a pair of scales around their necks. I made Pearl as comfortable as circumstances would allow, bathed the baby, dressed him in his second-hand clothing and placed him snugly in the laundry basket. Alma leaned over it and said, to nobody in particular, 'Poor li'le lad.'E didn't ask to be born, did 'e?' Then almost as if she was pleased, ''E's a bit like our Mark when 'e was a baby.' She lifted the corner of her apron, wiped her eyes and announced, 'Ah'll brew up, we could all do with a drink after that little lot.'

I followed her into the scullery, for there was a deal of cleaning up to be done. I noticed that Charlie kept hovering in the passage, as if he felt he should do something, but was uncertain what. I thought I knew the reason: he wanted to see the result of all the fuss. When I asked him if he would like to take a look at the baby, his face lit up, 'Aye, ah would that, if it's alreet by you like.' He stepped into the parlour, carefully keeping his back towards Pearl, and haunched down by the laundry basket. He made a few clicking noises with his tongue and said, 'What a downright ruddy shame. Poor little bastard.' Then, as if ashamed of his words and mood, he grasped a tiny little fist.

'Oo's a bonnie lad then?' he queried.

Chapter Two

One Monday morning in April 1954 I found myself standing in a queue at Burrowdale Labour Exchange. When I reached the counter, I asked the clerk if there were any vacancies for members of the nursing profession. She directed me to another clerk, and I waited in another queue. When my turn came I gave my name and my qualifications, saying that I was a state registered nurse and a certified midwife. Judging from the expression that flitted over her face, and from the vacancy cards that were produced it was obvious that a large number of nurses were needed in the area. Quickly, and without giving any reason, I told her that on no account would I consider midwifery. That statement reduced the number of cards, and after sifting through the remainder we found that there was a vacancy for a district nurse, for general nursing duties only; so I decided to apply.

After a quick phone call I was told that I had an appointment in an hour's time with a Mrs Elizabeth Macintosh, Superintendent of the Burrowdale District Nursing Association. Since the address I was given for the Nursing Centre was close to the Labour Exchange, I decided to have a cup of coffee and to reflect on the decision I had taken.

My thoughts went back over my nursing career. I remembered how my first step had been made about a month after I had had the row with Paul Mulholland. My heart had been broken and I knew I wouldn't be able to piece it together again unless I got away from him and Belfast; every place I went to, every friend I met, was a reminder of him. I thought at first of trying to heal the breach between us, but young as I was I knew that it was something that could only be patched, that throughout our lives it would continue until it became a permanent wound, so that our marriage would be bound to end in unhappiness and failure. I realized it was no good discussing a nursing career with my parents and so I went to an aunt whom I knew I could trust. She helped me write for particulars and forms, and acted as a post office on my behalf.

Eventually I was accepted as a student nurse at the North Middlesex Hospital in London. I then confronted my parents with what I thought was a *fait accompli*. They didn't think so. According to them I was breaking up the family group and behaving like a coward by running away from a situation I had created. They told me that London was one huge brothel, and that I would inevitably become a scarlet woman (this was a mistake on their part, as I'd always wondered what a brothel was

22

like and I was sufficiently confident of myself to know that while I might become light pink, given the chance, that was the brightest colour I would settle for). I stood my ground. Then the parish priest was called in to use his persuasive powers; he ended by saying that I was not worldly enough yet. I couldn't resist asking him what I had to do to become worldly – it threw him off his balance. Eventually, when it became clear to him that there was no likelihood of persuading me to change my mind, he gave me his blessing. He must have spoken to mum and dad, for gradually their attitude softened. This almost made me have second thoughts and, when the day came for me to leave home, it was with a heavy heart that I sailed from Belfast.

When I reached the nurses' home at the North Middlesex, it was quite different from what I'd expected. I'd imagined a sort of prison-like, Victorian brick mausoleum; instead I found a modern, four-storied, horse-shoe shaped building, light and airy. The entrance hall was large, bright and colourful, with glass display cabinets, from which, I found later, nurses could choose cosmetics, books, stationery, all the work-a-day things a girl requires; it was here also that we collected messages and our mail, and so was a precious contact with the outside world.

A large mosaic corridor led off the entrance hall. The right side of the corridor was lined with glass sliding doors, behind which there was a huge dining hall set out with small tables, stretching from the serving hatch to the end of the hall. The nurses were allotted to these tables in order of seniority. The six assistant matrons sat at the near tables, alongside four tutors; then came the ward sisters, in blue dresses, white aprons, navy-blue shoulder capes and the large army square head-dresses; then the staff nurses, in white with navy-blue epaulettes and belts; and finally the student nurses, from third to first year, had the tables that extended to the bottom of the hall. A far corner was reserved for the midwifery staff, since the North Middlesex, as well as training nurses, had a school for midwives. The midwifery staff kept themselves apart from the general nurses, not out of a sense of superiority, but because of the risk of infection from contact with those who worked in the wards. This I found a pity, since we were seldom able to get to know each other.

Past the dining hall there were the staff offices, and continuing round there were doors leading to the lecture and study rooms, and the three large sitting rooms reserved for the use of the student nurses and their friends. The left-hand side of the corridor was made up of glass windows, looking out onto a swimming pool and four hard tennis courts. In a way it had the appearance of a holiday hotel, but appearances could be deceptive, as I was to find out later.

At the end of the corridor a wide staircase led to the three upstairs floors, to the bedrooms and bathrooms. Again the sleeping accommodation was arranged in order of seniority. Student nurses had rooms on the first floor; the second more luxuriously housed the sisters and staff nurses, while the top floor was reserved for night sisters, night staff and student nurses. Whoever designed the building must have known something of the state of nurses when they come off duty, for there were three lifts to carry us to our respective floors.

It was a few days after my twentieth birthday when I entered this building that was to be my home for the next three years. I was one of eighty-four girls of more or less the same age who arrived that day, sharing the same ambition: to become a state registered nurse. Sixty of us realized this ambition, the other twenty-four dropped by the wayside.

As each bewildered newcomer arrived, she was welcomed by a Miss Taylor, the sister tutor, a tall, elegant, grey-haired lady, dressed in a neat fitting navy-blue uniform, trimmed with white lace. On her head was a well-starched frilly white cap, which tied under her chin in a bow of equally well-starched ribbons. She was a motherly sort of woman, which was just as well, since she was *in loco parentis* over us all. She not only taught us the rudiments of nursing but advised us on our general behaviour. 'Never go up to the West End alone, always in groups. When you start work on the wards you will find it very, very hard, tiring and often frustrating, so it is important not to skip meals, and to ensure that you have an adequate amount of sleep. To be able to look after sick people, you must be able to look after yourselves.' These were some of her warnings.

She had the tenderness of a mother, as we found, for she nursed us when we were ill; and she saw to it when she was teaching us that we learnt that there was a 'fun' side to nursing.

After our welcome we were taken to one of the nurses' sitting rooms, where we were supplied with and fitted into our uniforms – heavy white dresses, buttoned from the waist upwards, and covering white coats, again buttoned from the chin to the hemline. Our funny little white starched caps were gathered in pleats at the back, and rucked out to give the appearance of butterfly wings. When I looked at myself in the mirror I wasn't sure whether to laugh or cry at the odd-looking figure that gazed back at me. I felt like handing in my uniform and saying, 'I'm sorry, I don't think it's for me, I'll try somewhere else,' then taking the first train back to Ireland. However, as I watched the others struggling with the same gear and the same emotions, and looking equally astonished at their reflections in the mirror, I decided to give it a fair trial.

Some two hours later, eighty-four brand new student nurses, trying to look at ease in their uniforms, assembled in the dining hall to be addressed by Matron, a commanding figure, in yet another navy-blue dress, trimmed with lace, and a different styled army square on her head. As she spoke she emphasized the high standard of nursing that was the pride of the hospital, and how she expected us to maintain this standard, indeed, even to improve upon it. Her quiet cultured tones reminded me of my former headmistress, but behind them I detected a strength and fire that Sister Benedict lacked.

From that moment we were known as PTS (Preliminary Training School) nurses. For the next three months we spent our days in classrooms, starting at eight each morning, and our evenings studying in our rooms. We learned to work in groups of three or four; that way we were less inclined to fall asleep over our books. It was a habit I continued throughout my training. We got to know each other well. There were English, Welsh and Scots girls, and a large contingent from the Irish Free State; I was the only one who came from Northern Ireland. Few of us had set foot in London before, it had not been a place to visit during the war years, and most of us were a long way from home. I found this a good thing, for if ever I felt homesick there were plenty of others feeling the same way to cheer me up.

At the end of my first month I joined the pay queue outside the matron's office. We went in singly. As one girl came out, another knocked at the door and waited for the command to enter. When my turn came I walked towards Matron, who was sitting in a small armchair studying a sheet of paper spread out on her desk. A grey-haired hospital steward stood at the side of this chair, with a pile of pound notes in front of him, together with stacks of silver and copper coins. Matron lifted her head and said, 'Good morning, nurse, what is your name?' When I replied she ran her finger down the sheet of paper, then stopped and said, 'Sign here, please.' The steward then handed me one pound. That was my salary for a full month's work. I later found that if there were only thirty days in the month we were given nineteen shillings and fourpence.

I found it almost impossible to manage on so little, and told my mother so in my letters home. Without consulting my father she sent me the odd pound or so each month, then one day my father wrote reprimanding me for accepting this money. The gist of his letter was, 'You have made your bed, you must lie on it.' I knew mother must have had the sharp edge of his tongue, but to my relief it made no difference, her generosity continued. The only trouble was that I was unable to thank her for it.

At the end of our three months' study period, we were allocated to the wards as student nurses. If we thought we'd been hard worked previously we were very much mistaken. Now ward duty began at seven o'clock and generally ended at five-thirty. Two days a week we worked through until eight-thirty in the evening. Then there were lectures to be attended and studying to be done; now, some of us did fall asleep, even though we were working in groups. We were allowed a half day off each week, and a full day once a month.

My first assignment was to a men's medical ward. I quickly discovered that the greater part of a Cockney's sense of humour is founded on sex and the behaviour of certain parts of the anatomy. I also found that the more you reacted to their remarks and actions, the harder they drove you. It took me about a week to learn to live with them; after this I was able to counter their quips by replying in broad Irish, and pretending that I was as unable to understand them as they were me.

Even in those days there were jokes against the Irish, though not so plentiful, I'm glad to say, as they are today. I learnt to think fast. One evening a man asked for a bottle. I directed his attention to the one in the cabinet at the side of his bed. 'No, I want a hot-water bottle,' then he put his hand to his mouth and said, 'Sorry, nurse, I forgot you don't have such things in Ireland. You put a pig at the bottom of the bed to keep your feet warm.' I was ready for him.

'Quite right,' I replied. 'We don't have alarm clocks either, we put a rooster on the bed rail, tell him when we want a call, and bang on time he crows and wakes us up. Then he and the pig go to the kitchen, make a pot of tea, and bring it to us in bed. You see, our Irish animals are cleverer than English people.'

Even the doctors would occasionally pick on me. I remember one young houseman shouting from the middle of the ward, 'Can't you close the door? Oh I forgot, nurse, you don't have doors in Ireland, do you?'

'Oh yes, doctor, we do,' I retorted, 'but in my house I was accustomed to having a butler to open and shut them for me.'

At the end of my first year's training, and after I'd taken the preliminary examination, I was able to return to Ireland for a month's holiday. My feelings were mixed. I still loved my parents and my home, in spite of my father's intransigent attitude, but I was afraid both he and my mother would start the old pressures, try to make me give up my nursing career, and that therefore the four weeks would be spent in constant wranglings. I was wrong. My parents had compromised, and their concern now was that at the end of my training I would return to Belfast and work in a hopsital there. I made no promises. I found that my year in hospital had given me a new kind of presence, an authority and assurance. I was now a person in my own right, and I think my parents recognized this too.

By the end of my second year's training I had had experience in every ward of the hospital, as well as three months' theatre and out-patients duty. I then found myself back in the men's medical ward where I'd started my training, this time on night duty. Leading off the main ward were two smaller rooms. One, of two beds, was reserved for seriously ill patients and the other, of four beds, was kept for the 'gastrics', patients who were suffering from duodenal and peptic ulcers. One night as the day nurse handed me the ward report, she pointed to a new 'gastric' name, Colin Jordan, aged twenty-three, who was undergoing what we called the 'swill treatment'. This was an intra-gastric feed, delivered from a bottle by a tube passed from the throat to the stomach. When I entered the ward that evening I little dreamed that the quiet, brown-haired, brown-eyed new patient, with a Ryles tube in his left nostril, and head buried in a book, was to become my husband.

The three other patients were laughing and joking in their usual way, but the new patient just carried on reading. When I'd finished filling his feed bottle I asked him how he was feeling.

'A'm champion,' he replied. His accent was strange in what was primarily a hospital for Londoners. Thinking he might be lonely, I tried to get him to talk some more, but the others monopolized me with their banter and chatter, so it wasn't until the following night that he told me he came from Burrowdale.

'Where's that?' I asked.

'Near Rabbitsville,' came from the wit in the next bed.

It took me about a week to get the briefest of life histories from Colin, to find that he was an electrical engineer working for a contract firm in London, that he was staying with his married brother and his wife in Enfield, and that he was looking forward to returning to his beloved home town. As his condition improved so, to a degree, did his powers of conversation, though by comparison he remained quiet and unassuming. Despite his reserve I felt drawn in some way to him and, as the time for his discharge from hospital drew nearer, I knew I would miss him more than any other patient I had nursed previously. He left without saying good-bye to me. I was angry and hurt when I looked into his ward that night to find an empty bed, and then later when a new patient was admitted in his place I looked on him almost as an intruder.

How Colin discovered that I had two nights off duty due to me I've never been able to find out, but about a week after he had left he wrote inviting me to meet him outside the hospital on the first of these two nights. It was the beginning of a new life for me; from now on I didn't have to plan how I would spend my time off duty, it was done for me. I met his brother Jeff and his wife Ruth, and now found I had a home in London. A less shy Colin told me the intimacies of his life: that he had a great love of the country, and a fondness for animals, enjoyed dancing and liked a drink. Marriage was never mentioned, though it was obvious that he envied his brother's home life. One day, walking on Hampstead Heath, he told me that his contract was ending the following week, and that he would be returning home.

'When you're up in Burrowdale I'll take you along the beaches with Trixie and Bess.' This promised walk with his two fox terriers was the only sign I got that our relationship was to continue. I didn't need to worry; he wrote to me regularly and made frequent visits to London, and even if there were no outward signs from him that he wanted to establish a permanent relationship, his brother gave them on his behalf, for I was still expected to spend my off-duty time with them.

It was after I had sat my final examination in 1948 that I eventually saw Burrowdale, and met Colin's mother and father. My visit and lasting impression of them were of warmth, welcome and 'take us as we are'. Colin's mother was small and with the brown eyes that he had inherited. His father was a tall, impressive man and, like Colin, a little withdrawn at first meeting. There were two younger children, a brother and a sister, both at grammar school. As I've said, there was no fuss or formality, and already it seemed to me that I was one of the family.

Burrowdale as a town at first seemed both uninviting and unattractive. The shops were dull and ordinary compared with those of Belfast or London. I missed the bustle and excitement of city life. The dances reminded me of village hops, and the cinemas of flea pits. It wasn't until Colin and I walked with the dogs on the unspoiled beaches, and took trips to Windermere and Ambleside, that I caught the feeling of freedom, the colour, the light, the sense of unity, which the surroundings gave. I met the people and found them unsophisticated, natural and warm-hearted. So when three days before the holiday ended Colin asked me to marry him, I had no hesitation in saying, 'Yes.' There had to be conditions, and some may say that these took the romance out of our relationship.

Nursing, for me, had become so much more than a job, it was now my life's inspiration. I had little doubt that I'd passed my Finals and I wanted the opportunity to practise as a staff nurse what I'd learned over the past three years. I also felt that I could only become a complete nurse if I qualified as a midwife, and this would mean a further year's training. It would therefore be at least two years before we could get married; this was my stipulation. Colin however raised no objections, though he suggested that I did my midwifery training at the local maternity hospital, and I readily agreed. There was one other problem, that of religion. Colin was a Protestant, and although I made no stand, it was a comfort to me that he decided to enter the Catholic faith.

When I returned to London I was told that I had been successful in my Finals. Sixty new state registered nurses assembled outside the principal tutor's office, to be first congratulated and then deflated: 'Well done! Now you can start learning what nursing is all about.'

I rang my parents to tell them. My father was not impressed: 'Now that you've got that nonsense off your chest, you'll be able to come back home.' It was the opportunity to break my big news to him, 'I'll be coming back for a holiday in three months' time, bringing my husband-to-be with me.' I could feel the silence at the other end of the line, so I made a few noises about having to get back on duty, and put the phone down before he had a chance to comment. I knew though that the cat was amongst the pigeons in our house in Belfast.

As the time for Colin's and my visit grew nearer, the greater was my concern about how we would be greeted. I need not have worried, their attitude towards me had changed; in their eyes I was now a woman in my own right. This made it possible for me to alter my plans, and so in some measure to satisfy my parents. I decided to take a job as a staff nurse in a Belfast hospital for a time, and enjoy this new home that I had found.

The transition from student to staff nurse had come easily, but when I joined the Musgrave Park Hospital and found that since the sister was on prolonged sick leave I was in charge of a men's ward of forty-two patients, all suffering from tuberculosis, I had more than a few butterflies in my stomach.

I don't know whether it was because they thought that I was English – 'The wee staff nurse from across the water', for apparently I had now completely lost my accent; or whether it was because I borrowed the script of the sister on the first male medical ward I had worked on as a student, 'Now, gentlemen, you are in hospital to be made well again. We are all trying to see that your recovery is as complete as can be, but without your co-operation our job will be impossible. So please stop behaving like children' – but they obeyed me without argument, and indeed were generally profuse in their apologies, to which I replied with a cool 'Thank you'.

One blond boy of about my own age began following me about the ward. Wherever I went he seemed to appear: in the kitchen, the clinical room, or the sluice. One day he came into the office and without any preliminaries burst out, 'See here now, I know you're English, but that doesn't matter to me. I think a lot of you, so I do. Will you marry me when I leave here?' If he hadn't been so earnest I'd have had difficulty in not laughing. I explained that I was engaged to be married, thanked him for what I considered a great compliment, and then told him that I was born and brought up not ten minutes' walk from his own home. Though I'd been as gentle with him as I knew how, he looked hurt and bewildered, 'It's not fair, there's no ring on your finger.' I told him that jewellery was something nurses didn't wear. He seemed to understand; he moved towards the door, then turned, and with a smile said, 'It's some comfort anyway to know you're not English.'

In February 1950, almost a year to the day that I had joined there, I left Musgrave Park, Belfast, and went as a student midwife to the Burrowdale Maternity Hospital. The ''Allo, luv, you must be one of t'new nurses' that the maid greeted me with made me realize straight away my loss of status. It was also reflected by the severe cut in my salary. As a staff nurse I'd been getting fourteen pounds a month, and this was now reduced to five.

The hospital was very small, more like a large Victorian house, and catered for only forty-eight patients. As a result it was more friendly, the matron had none of the austere, distant qualities I'd learned to associate with the rank, she was a 'one of the girls' type of woman, but none the worse for that. She combined the duties of matron and tutor, so that I and the other four nurses who'd joined with me quickly got to know her well.

Although it was a small hospital, it was a busy one: before our final examination at the end of the six months' course we were expected to have delivered twenty babies; I had delivered eighty. It was, I suppose, Burrowdale's contribution to the post-war population explosion. We took our babies seriously. They were not just bundles that gulped milk in at one end and let it out at the other; to us they were little human beings that we'd had a part in bringing into the world.

Although the work was hard and the hours long, Colin and I were able to enjoy six months of courtship. I saw him most evenings and visited his home frequently. When we had a day off together we would go to Coniston where, without regard for the weather, we would row on the lake, afterwards visiting The Crown for hot soup on cold days, and cool shandy on hot days. This way of life had to come to an end, and after yet another examination I moved to the Sharoe Green Hospital at Preston, for my Part Two training.

Now I was one of thirty students. Much of the work concerned the legal aspects of district midwifery, and the rules laid down by the Central Midwives' Board. Deliveries there were more difficult to come by and we would hover in flocks around the labour wards like vultures waiting to swoop. The mothers-to-be must have felt more important than the Queen when they were in labour.

There was, however, one poor mother whom nobody wanted to know. It was the first, and only, time I came into contact with a syphilitic patient.

She was admitted during the night, with what were

described as vague pains, and she was still having them at seven-thirty in the morning, when I went on duty. She was lying in one of the four beds in the receiving ward. Orders had been issued that no other mothers-to-be were allowed in with her, and that she was not to go further into the hospital, but was to be delivered on that bed, and in that ward. Her baby was to be left with her, and within eight hours of the birth she was to be transferred by ambulance to the Preston Isolation Hospital.

Not another student midwife was to be seen in the vicinity of her ward that morning. I was doing a split duty and had time off between one and four. I had to look at the patient before I left, and from the way things seemed to be going it looked as though all would be over by the time I returned, and the baby safely tucked in its cot.

It didn't work out that way. I came back to find the patient screaming; a midwifery sister, dressed in white wellingtons, a mackintosh apron, with a rubber cap pulled over her eyebrows, leaving just a slit for her eyes between it and her mask, and wearing an extra thick pair of rubber gloves, was trying desperately to administer gas and air from a distance of four feet. On the bed in the next cubicle was a similar set of protective clothing, which the sister gestured me to put on.

We worked together for about an hour, with no result. At five-thirty the sister went off duty, and I was left there on my own. The heat from the clothing, and from the situation in which I found myself, was intense and, when the time finally came to deliver, I thought I would collapse, since I now had to wear a sterile gown over everything else.

There were none of the usual willing hands to help me. One nurse did present me with a bath of carbolic lotion, from outside the curtain, and gave me instructions to put the bed linen in it immediately the delivery was over. When at last the baby arrived, I nearly cried with grief as I bathed it, for it was born with sores on its body and the typical saddle nose that would identify it for what it was for life. I did everything for the mother and child with mechanical robot-like movements. All feeling seemed to be sapped from my mind and body. When it was over I emerged from the ward and stood with arms limp, tears mingled with sweat trickling into my mask.

'Get out of those things immediately.' The midwifery superintendent's order brought me to my senses. I went into the bathroom opposite the ward, and did as she'd instructed. 'Now you will go off duty, have a bath, wash your hair in a strong Savlon solution, and return here with every item of clothing you have been wearing, including your stockings and underclothes, these you will then take to the incinerator, and burn. Thank you for carrying out so successfully what I hope will be the most unpleasant duty you will ever have to perform here.'

Many of my friends and colleagues have shown astonishment when I have told them this story. It should be remembered that the incident occurred over twenty-five years ago, when antibiotics were in their infancy. Also this patient had booked in very late so that the penicillin treatment which could normally have been administered during the ante-natal period, and which might well have spared the infection from being transmitted to her child, had not been given.

There is too a widespread belief that any venereal disease cannot be contracted except through sexual intercourse. This is not true in the case of syphilis, since the contact of a cut or wound with a syphilitic sore can transfer the microbe *Treponeme Pallidum*.

It is of particular importance in a maternity hospital that the patients whose uteruses are generally raw and vulnerable to any infection should be particularly protected. Hence what may seem super-cautious procedures were regarded by those on the spot as ordinary and essential safeguards.

Those of us who had looked after the patient were worried as to how she would react when her condition and that of the baby were explained to her. The hospital registrar gave a short but sympathetic description of what had happened. It was delivered with kindness and tact, and she assured the mother that everything possible would be done at the Isolation Hospital to bring them both back to full health. The patient listened attentively, and when the registrar had concluded by asking if she had any questions, she replied eagerly, 'Yes, what will the visiting hours be there?'

Once again, after three months at Preston, my efforts were rewarded, but I still had another course to take to complete Part Two; I had to be attached to a district midwife, recognized as suitable to teach her trade to those who wished to learn it. We were allowed to choose which area we wanted to go to, and I decided on Morecambe, since it was near to Burrowdale, and Colin.

For my last month at Preston I was on night duty. During this outline of my training I have tried not to stress the tensions that the hours, and sometimes the conditions of work, put upon nurses. Often these were hard, but generally they were just. Discipline might seem petty at the time, but on reflection it was possible to see its purpose. To any persistent grousers I had one reply, 'If you find it's that bad, why don't you finish with it and get out?' To join the nursing profession you don't need to have a vocation – to stay with it, you do. Nevertheless there are occasions when even the most dedicated have doubts, and the one that I most particularly remember began on my last night on duty at Preston.

I worked solidly from eight in the evening to seven in the morning. I went to my room to snatch a few hours' sleep before catching my train at three that afternoon for Morecambe only to find that my bed had been stripped and to be told by the maid that the beds were being prepared for a new batch of students, and that if I was that tired I could sleep in a chair in the sitting room. There was little chance with the to-ings and fro-ings that were going on, nor could I snatch any sleep on the train, as there were two changes. At Morecambe I was met by a plump, rosy-cheeked, busy Dorothy Holmes, in her grey and blue district midwife's uniform. She greeted me with a beaming smile, and said, 'You're in luck, I've got a case in the first stage, she should deliver later on tonight.' I could have cried. All I wanted to do was to creep into bed. Instead I was whipped round to my lodgings, where the landlady offered the cup of tea I was longing for. 'We've no time for that, I'm afraid, we've a confinement to attend to.' Off I was whisked, with a chattering Dorothy Holmes bombarding me with questions and instructions, as we drove through the foulest of nights, with the tide lashing over the sea wall and a driver who was oblivious to the conditions, and indeed to any of the other unfortunate road users. Fear was now added to the other emotions I was experiencing. I sent up a thank-you prayer to God when we reached our destination, then threw myself out of the car to follow the already disappearing midwife.

I must say, from what I remember, the surroundings were delightful and the patient, a woman of about forty, apologetic about bringing us out on such a night. Nurse Holmes took over straight away. My brain was reeling, as opening her nursing bag, she produced piece by piece its contents, and described the function and purpose of each one. I followed on her heels as she moved quickly into the kitchen with the bowls and instruments, and showed me how they should be boiled. She heated the carrycot with a hot-water bottle, fussed over the baby things, all the time shooting questions at me, and at the patient, until neither of us knew who was expected to answer what. Give her her due, she achieved what I suppose was her objective, for the first stage of labour progressed into the second stage without any trouble. As the labour pains grew more frequent and fierce, she launched into a long conversation about cake making, something at which the patient apparently excelled, and as she gasped her replies the nurse would either prompt her or query, 'What was that? How much flour did you say you use? How hot should the oven be?'

It was as ludicrous as sitting in a dental chair, mouth wedged open, with that pipe thing sucking away at the saliva and a garrulous dentist asking questions that even if you were capable of answering, you wouldn't want to. Yet Mary, for that I'd gathered was the patient's name, seemed to enjoy it. She would come out of a spasm of pain, which had robbed her temporarily of speech, and take up from where she'd left off. When the time came for us to scrub, Dorothy Holmes told me to take over, 'Just carry on, my dear, as if you were in hospital. Babies don't come any different whether it's in a palace or a pig sty, do they, Mary dear?' Mary just grunted, perhaps because she was unsure what category her house was being put into. Nurse Holmes held her leg, and as she continued chattering away the baby appeared. It's my opinion she talked it into the world; whatever it was, it was the easiest delivery I had ever performed, and strangely, despite the fact that I'd had no sleep for forty-eight hours, on the baby's arrival I no longer felt tired.

The drive back was no less hazardous than the journey there, but I adopted a fatalistic attitude. There were, I knew, likely to be many such journeys during the next three months, so I might as well get accustomed. Dorothy Holmes's 'Goodnight, Patricia, see you at eight' when we reached my lodgings reminded me that I would have four precious hours in bed before starting again. Sleep didn't come easily, babies and cars rushed behind my closed eyelids as though they were on a production line, and for the first time in my nursing career I murmured to myself, 'There must be some other way of earning a living.'

As I've said I had chosen Morecambe because it was near Burrowdale but I might just as well have been in Timbuctoo, for not once was I able to leave there. Colin came to see me twice. The first time he got to know my landlady and her husband, the Sawyers, well, for no sooner had he arrived than I was called out on an emergency, and by the time it was over he had had to leave to catch his train. The next time we were both free I decided to make myself scarce. I met him in a little pub, Davy Jones Locker. I had to leave a note saying where I was, but we spent a cheery, undisturbed evening together. The following morning, round came Nurse Holmes in high dudgeon, and proceeded to lambast me in front of the Sawyers for gross unprofessional conduct. 'You missed a case,' she said. I explained that I had left an address where I could be contacted, whereupon she blew up, 'I would not demean myself by calling for you at a public house. You have disgraced your uniform by going into such a place.' I told her I had not been in my uniform; it still made no difference, in her eyes I was a leper.

When she left, Mr Sawyer got to his feet, walked over to the sideboard, took a bottle of brandy from the cupboard and poured two measures from it. 'Get yersel on the outside o' this, luv, and tak no notice of that hypocritical bitch.' I began to protest about it being too early to drink. 'It's medicine lass, go on, treat thesen.' He was right, it was.

Eventually the longest three months of my life came to an end. Once again I sat for an examination, once again I passed. I returned to the Burrowdale Maternity Hospital as a staff midwife. I had achieved my vocational ambition. In April 1951 Colin and I were married, in my parish church in Belfast. I could now devote myself to my husband, and to leading a full life. I continued to work for over a year, but it was at a slower tempo now that I was practising what I'd been taught. I was promoted to midwifery sister within a few months. Colin's and my life blended together, the waiting, the snatched meetings seemed to have added to our eventual happiness. It was with great joy, therefore, that early in 1953 I found I was pregnant. I continued to work until June, and my leaving party from the hospital was not one of farewell, since as an ante-natal patient I should be making regular appearances.

It was sixteen weeks after I had left there that I was readmitted to the hospital. It is strange, and perhaps ironic, that something I and the hospital staff had looked forward to as a joyous occasion should have to end so harshly and unfairly. You can know so much, yet you really know nothing until you have produced a baby of your own.

My labour began at half-past-seven in the morning. I decided that I was not going to be one of those mothers who rush to hospital when they feel the first twinges. I wasn't going to be alone in a labour ward for hours. I would be ready to deliver when I arrived. It was five o'clock in the evening before I left home. I spent another seven hours in hospital, suffering severe pains, before it was decided to perform a caesarian operation. I had a son, who weighed seven pounds; yes, even I found I was interested in his weight. Tragically, and partly as a result of my own 'cleverness', the baby had a sub-tentorial haemorrhage, a torn covering of the brain, through my being in labour too long. He had been pushing his head down and because I had a rigid cervix he hadn't been able to reach the light.

David, for so he was christened, lived only six weeks, despite the efforts of the staff of the Leeds General Hospital, where he was transferred. For me, as a mother and a midwife, it was a disaster, something that was to affect me deeply in the months to come. To some degree I was comforted by the fact that there was no discernible reason why I should not have a baby in the future, but nevertheless, within me was a deep sense of failure. Perhaps it was premonition, for after two miscarriages, in 1958 and 1961, it became apparent that motherhood was to be denied me.

It took me about six months to recover my balance. By that I don't mean that I became a neurotic wreck, but it was only after this period of time that I felt I could face the world on equal terms. I decided to return to nursing, but I also determined that it would not be in an area where I would be called upon to deliver, or even handle, babies. It was this decision that was responsible for my visit to the Labour Exchange, and why I was now drinking coffee before being interviewed for the position of district nurse.

Chapter Three

The District Nurses' Home, as it was called at that time, was a large converted house standing in its own grounds, and situated in a tree-lined avenue off Helmsdale Road, the main road leading out of the town and up into the hills. At the time it was built it had formed part of the outskirts of the town, but with the development that had taken place was now considered as being almost in the centre.

As I walked up the drive, I was surprised to see curtains hanging over the windows; in hospitals they had always been considered as a source of infection. The door was answered by a young girl, whose head and shoulders protruded towards me, as if she was waiting to get into a rugby scrum. I explained the reason for my call and with a 'Follow me, please' she turned on her heels and, head and shoulders leading scurrying feet, she swept down a corridor. I followed hot-a-foot. She stopped suddenly at the bottom of a staircase, pointed to a chair, and with a 'Sit there, please' set off up the stairs at the double, her head almost brushing the carpet. I heard the sounds of doors opening and closing, and bursts of rapid footsteps, then there she was again, halfway down the stairs. 'Mrs Macintosh is nowhere to be found,' she hissed in a stage whisper, 'she must be at the top of the house.' She made a rude gesture with her fingers, about-turned and followed their direction.

I was beginning to take stock of my surroundings, when I heard raised voices from above. A Scottish one boomed out, 'Well, who is she, and what does she want?'

'She said—'

'Never mind what she said, ah'll soon find out.'

Then a large female figure appeared at the top of the stairs. She stopped and looked down at me, through rimless glasses.

'Well, and what do ye want?' she barked.

'I've come—'

'Wait a minute, can't you see ah'm coming doon.'

'She's an ogress,' I thought. I'd heard that there were some in the nursing profession, though up to now I'd never met one. She reached the bottom of the stairs and stood over me.

'Now,' she said, as if giving me permission to speak.

I rose and gazed into her bosom. 'I've been sent about a vacancy you have for a district nurse,' I began.

'What!' She turned to the luckless clerk, 'Why didn't ye tell me so, and why, may ah ask, has this nurse been kept sitting in the corridor – she should have been shown into my office straight away. Off with ye, and prepare a tray of tea.' Away the poor girl went, head and shoulders drooping even lower. I was later to learn that my sympathy for her was wasted; like Atlas, she had been supporting Mrs Mac for many years, enjoyed her work and was devoted to her mistress.

The superintendent, for that was Mrs Mac's official title, now turned her attention to me. She became all sweetness and light as she steered me to her office. She lowered me into a chair opposite her desk, and sat down facing me. Then came the usual questions, name, address, schooling, and as we went through my training she seemed almost to purr. 'There must indeed be a shortage of district nurses,' I thought. When I told her my reason for leaving my last post as sister at the maternity hospital, of the tragedy that followed and my determination never to return to midwifery, she gazed at me with sad, spaniel-like eyes and seemed to hang on every word. As I came to the end of my story her face twitched. 'Oh heavens!' I thought, 'she's going to cry.' I couldn't have borne it, I would have had to rush from the building, I couldn't stand any more sympathy; indeed, my purpose in coming here was to get away from that kind of thing. I needn't have worried; her face gradually reset itself, she rose to her feet and made for the side door of her office. 'Are ye going to be all day bringing that tea?' she roared through it.

'Coming, coming,' replied a voice. It was as if the clerk had been waiting for a rebuke before bringing it.

We continued talking through two cups of tea, with

Mrs Mac describing the kind of work that I would be doing, making it sound more rewarding than any other kind of nursing except, of course, financially; my monthly wage would be £10 less than I had been getting as a ward sister. I noticed that whenever she became emotional or tense she rattled her Rs with her tongue, flicking her top teeth. 'I shall know the kind of mood to expect when I hear that in future,' I thought to myself. I later discovered that I was not alone in my thinking; one of the senior doctors of the town almost caused a major incident. It was in the doctors' club, and Mrs Mac was a guest at some function there; as usual she was making her presence felt by arguing a point among a group of doctors. This particular doctor could stand it no longer, 'Don't you roll your arse at me,' he cried. As so often happens there was dead silence in the room, and everyone turned round to see the red-faced pair confronting each other. All power to Mrs Mac, she sensed the danger of the situation and roared with laughter, which everyone around was relieved to echo.

As a sop for the poor money that I was being offered, Mrs Mac brought the conversation round to the subject of transport. I explained that I hadn't a car, nor indeed did I know how to drive. 'Dinna fret yersel aboot that. I'll arrange for ye to tak lessons with the Corporation driving instructor, and it'll ney cost ye a halfpenny. After that ye'll allus be able to use one from the Corporation car pool.' Again, what she didn't mention was that those supplied to district nurses were the worn-out vehicles that nobody else would, or often could, drive. Many's the time I was on urgent call and was unable to find a car that would start, yet if ever I suggested using one reserved for a chairbound official to get to my suffering patient, it was as if I had blasphemed. It's this kind of narrow officialdom that seems to pervade anyone who works in local government service. It forced me to buy my own car as soon as I could possibly afford one.

It was arranged that I would start work on the Monday of the following week, and since it was now Thursday, I did protest that it was a little soon, but Mrs Mac brushed me aside, 'It'll be the best thing for ye, ye'll get yersel out of yersel, and that's what ye need.' She didn't mention that my extra pair of hands were going to be of help to her. 'We'll go now and fix ye up with a uniform, and then ah'll show ye the rest of the building.' We went upstairs, where I tried on a number of clothes, all of which were too big for me. When we came to the smallest that was in stock, Mrs Mac grabbed a handful of material at the back and pushed me in front of the mirror, 'There, that'll fit ye, though ye may have to tak it in a bit, and shorten it, but it suits ye fine.' I surrendered, though it took me the whole weekend to make anything of it.

We then explored the house. There was the district room, where the equipment was stored, very much like a clinical room in a hospital, except there were few instruments to be seen. There were twelve lockers which housed the nursing bags, the sign of our profession, and large cupboards containing the other essentials for a nurse's work: mackintosh sheets, bedpans and the like. The nearby assistant superintendent's office looked like a committee room, with its long table and twelve chairs. At the far end, in a bay window, was a large desk and along the wall was a bookcase divided into named sections; here were kept the case registers, category ledgers and books in which each nurse accounted for her hours of duty, and the condition of her patients. Finally, I was shown the common room, typical of any nurses' common room, with its sofas and easy chairs, writing desks and a table covered with the medical and nursing journals of months past. It was a comfortable room, where I was to spend many happy hours, for the friendship, loyalty and comradeship of district nurses was, I found, unmatched by any other branch of the service.

Our tour of duty over, Mrs Mac apologized that there were no nurses around for her to introduce me to. 'Some of them will be back in an hour,' she said, as if hoping that I would volunteer to stay and meet them. I'd had enough for one day; I felt overwhelmed and mentally exhausted. I looked at my watch as if making a decision, and then declared that I had better be getting back to my husband. 'Half-past-eight Monday morning, then,' she said, as I gathered up the parcel containing my ill-fitting uniform, and started for home wondering whether I'd made the right decision. 'What decision?' I suddenly asked myself. 'You made no decision, Mrs Mac made it for you.'

My first Monday morning was spent filling in the details of Mrs Mac's *spiel*. I was first introduced to the nurse who was to look after and initiate me during my early weeks 'on the district'.

Anne Evans was everybody's dream of what a nurse should look like; the picture on the recruiting poster a few years later was a carbon copy: a slim, trim girl with neatly bobbed hair, calm, smiling eyes, behind which lay the power of command, of efficiency and kindliness. Anne was able to persuade even the most indolent of her patients to prepare for her visits, so that their sick rooms, as we called them, were clean, the basin, boiling water, soap, towels were ready, and that there were tins in the kitchen to sterilize dressings and instruments. Where clean cloths were not available, newspapers were provided to protect the surfaces that she worked from. She was a perfectionist, a copy-book nurse, who seemed always to be able to work to the rules, something that I'm afraid I often found difficult, and sometimes impossible. Yet socially Anne was a loner, her charm and persuasive manner were confined to nursing; she could be curt to the point of rudeness outside her work. She studied two nights a week at evening classes, had no men friends, and kept away from our get-togethers or parties. She seemed unconscious of her appearance; as nurse 'Busty' Clarke often said, 'If I had her looks, wouldn't I turn them to my advantage, it's bloody unfair, that's what it is.'

'Busty' was another colleague to whom I was introduced that morning. Her nickname described her both physically and mentally. She was an excellent nurse, but tactless and inclined to burst out at the wrong moment and in the wrong places. She was great, but sometimes embarrassing, company.

Mrs Evelyn Telford was the assistant superintendent; she was tall and willowy. Her fair hair was always neatly arranged, though in a rather outdated chignon. She wore her uniform as though she had grown in it. Although a local girl, her accent was without the slightest trace of dialect, her voice was quiet and her carefully chosen words were pronounced slowly and deliberately. As I got to know her it seemed strange that she was subordinate to Mrs Mac. She had joined the Queen Alexandra's Nursing Corps after finishing her nurse's training at the beginning of the war, had nursed at front-line hospitals in the desert and later during the allied advances across Europe, and at the end of the war had held the rank of Lieutenant-Colonel. In 1944 she'd married an army officer, who was killed shortly afterwards in action. She could have had the pick of any of the top hospital jobs, but had elected to come to Burrowdale, so that she could be with her sick mother. It was our good fortune, for although she was a strict disciplinarian, she was fair and acted as a kind of buffer for the staff in their dealings with Mrs Mac, and her rantings and roarings. There was no doubt that Mrs Mac feared and respected her, as much as any of the nurses. 'Busty' Clarke was the only one of us who disliked her. They were of course complete opposites.

One hot summer's afternoon, a section of nurses had reported in about five o'clock to receive our evening duties. 'Busty' was late and, when she eventually arrived, her thick uniform coat was buttoned up to her chin, and she was sweating profusely. We nurses, of course, knew what had happened. A naval ship was in port and 'Busty' had been entertaining one of the crew; time had ceased to exist and she had eventually dashed out to receive her duties, meaning to return later to collect the rest of her clothes. She'd thought that Evelyn would by now have left the nurses' home.

When the assistant superintendent saw her, her blue eyes turned to steel.

'Nurse Clarke, open your coat, please.'

'Busty's' face went crimson, she clutched at the collar as if to protect herself.

'Why should I?' she cried defiantly.

'I'm waiting, Nurse Clarke, you will undo the buttons of your coat.'

'Busty' realized there was no way out. With tears rolling from her eyes she began undoing the buttons, exposing a lacy black bra, then she stopped.

'All the way down, nurse,' came the command.

It was like a sad striptease, as, fumbling with button after button, her navy-blue coat opened.

'Now take it off.' Evelyn Telford was relentless.

'Busty', now completely abject, threw it aside and stood in front of us, clad only in her black bra and the scantiest pair of black frilly knickers.

'Now you will replace your coat and return in half an hour, properly dressed for duty. Thank you.'

It was an offence for which 'Busty' might have been severely punished, even dismissed, but no more was said about the incident. I think Evelyn Telford felt she had suffered enough.

My first week with Anne Evans was one of the most fascinating of my career so far. Caring for a variety of patients in their own homes gave nursing another dimension, and the business of getting people back to full health, and not just well enough to leave hospital, was most rewarding. We dealt with people in all walks of life, young and old, poor and not so poor; the rich generally engaged private nurses, or went into nursing homes.

I began to get to know various sections of the community that made up the town of Burrowdale, as well as people in the surrounding farms and villages, and the fishermen on the coast. They were mostly warm-hearted and hospitable, grateful for the help you were giving them, and even the crotchety or the eccentric were either fun or a challenge. As I was nearing the end of my preliminary induction period, I began more and more to look forward to having my own list of patients, and becoming personally involved with them.

When the day came, I reported to Mrs Mac in the morning in a mood of high anticipation. As I went into her office I noticed that she had another, oldish, senior nurse with her. I began to apologize for having intruded.

'No, come on in, Patricia,' said Mrs Mac, her voice smooth and honeyed. 'Ah want to introduce ye to Miss Merrivale.' I made the usual noises. 'Miss Merrivale,' continued Mrs Mac, 'is superintendent of the district midwives.' A little red light shone in my mind. 'The poor lady is in great trouble, and it has always been oor practice in Burrowdale to help each other in an hour of need.' The red light grew brighter. Mrs Mac went blandly on, 'She has recently lost two of her midwives, and this morning another has reported sick, she is desperately in need of help.'

'But you'll remember I told you . . .' I interrupted.

'Ah know only too well what ye told me of your tragic experience,' Mrs Mac's face took on a sad, cow-like expression, 'and ah've taken the liberty of acquainting Miss Merrivale with some of the details, and she feels for ye, as ah do. But things have reached a point where personal feelings [and here she rolled her Rs] must give way to higher considerations, as I think ye will agree. Mind ye, the decision must be yours.'

Silently, I called her all the names under the sun; she was a common, blackmailing whore, but she had got me in a corner and there was no way out. 'Very well, it's against my wishes, I'll do it, but not for long.' There was a sound as of escaping steam as both ladies gave sighs of relief. I turned to Miss Merrivale, 'When do you want me to start?'

'There's no time like the present,' said Mrs Mac. As we left the room together I realized that I hadn't, as yet, heard Miss Merrivale speak a word.

The District Midwives Centre was only two houses away, and was similarly laid out to our own. There was one difference: the atmosphere was less friendly. Midwives worked from their homes and rarely got to know each other well. As I had learned the routine at Morecambe, I needed little instruction, it was merely a question of changing bags. By the early afternoon I was at home, look-ing at the telephone and waiting with apprehension for my first call. It was not long in coming. I almost snatched at the receiver as the bell began ringing. 'It's Doctor Fairlie, nurse,' a deep Scots voice announced. 'Ah don't think ah've had the pleasure of your acquaintance, though ah've heard ye're very highly qualified.' (I was not impressed. For the second time that day I knew I was being treated with an overdose of Scottish blarney.) I made no comment. This must have thrown the doctor, because after a second or two's pause he said, 'Are ye there, nurse?' I told him I was. 'Well, it's a poor wee patient of mine, a lady by the name of Pearl Caine, of 10 Old Street on the Westland Estate; she's starting labour. Ah'm sure it's a straightforward case, and ah'll be obliged if ye'll tak over.'

'Very well, doctor,' I replied, then asked a few questions, which seemed to bewilder him.

'Ah, weel, ah'm afraid I don't know a lot of detail. Ah suggested she contacted the maternity hospital, but this didn't seem to please. She's a rough diamond, given to using bad language, but ah'm sure ye're used to that, eh?' and he gave a slight chuckle. I didn't respond. 'Weel, ah'll leave her in your safe hands. Be sure to ring me if ye run into trouble, but ah'm certain ye won't. Good night to ye,' and he rang off. So did I, then I reached again for the phone, ordered a taxi, and set out for Pearl Caine and my first home delivery in Burrowdale.

Chapter Four

The morning after Pearl's delivery, I phoned Doctor Fairlie to make my report. There was, it seemed, a different person on the other end, there were none of the dulcet tones of the previous evening. His voice was brusque and his manner almost unfriendly. I'd only spoken a few words when he interrupted me, 'Ah don't like discussing patients on these infernal machines. If ye've anything to say to me, come and see me,' and he hung up.

'Very well, you Scottish humbug. I've plenty to say, so I will.'

This was to be the first of many journeys that I made to his house, The Priory, and generally in a similar mood to the one I was in now: determined to give him a piece of my mind and to try and make him realize he couldn't shelve his responsibilities. Always, as happened on this first day, I came away cursing myself for a fool, aware that he had charmed the pants off me and had turned every one of my implied criticisms aside, or used them to his own advantage.

'I know you're a very busy man, doctor, but—' I'd start.

'Ay, ay,' he'd break in, 'it's comforting, nurse, that ye realize how overworked ah am, and ah want ye to know how grateful ah am to ye and the other fine nursing ladies, for the way in which ye try to lighten my load. It's a hard calling is medicine, and it doesn't get any easier as ye get older.' He'd then straighten his back, as though relieving his aching bones.

'But you will promise to go and see the patient.'

'Promises, my dear lassie, are things ye learn niver to give, the longer ye live with medicine. We can only do our best; give hope, ay, promises, niver.'

'But I'm very worried—'

'Dinna fuss yersen, ye leave the worrying to me. Now what do ye think we should prescribe for that poor owd body?' He would then write out a prescription. 'Now go with that to the pharmacist, and have it made up. Och, and while ye're at it, ye may as well tak these others, and perhaps ye'd be kind enough to deliver them, it'll save me a journey.'

He mixed charm, humour and pathos; you left him with warmth and love in your heart. It was only as the cold light of reason took over that you realized that you'd been outwitted and out-manoeuvred once again.

I wasn't alone in the relationship I had with him. All the other nurses experienced the same thing; only Mrs Mac was able to cope. If ever in desperation we put our case to her, she was delighted to take it up. 'Ah'll soon shift that lazy, awkward Aberdonian,' she'd say, lifting the phone.

'Och, so ye're theer then,' she'd begin, 'noo ye can shift yer fat sen, and git roond and see some of yer patients. Here is a list of a few,' and she'd rattle off names and addresses. 'Ah'll ring ye during surgery hours and find oot how ye got on, and to give ye another list. Be off wi' ye.' She'd slam the phone down in glee. 'The feckless awd sinner. I luv him,' she'd murmur.

Doctor Robert Fairlie MB, FFPSG (Bachelor of Medicine, Fellow of the Faculty of Physicians and Surgeons, Glasgow), to give him his full titles, was known to all as the Laird. He was tall, broad-shouldered, with a bushy moustache which like his unruly mop of coarse hair was in the process of turning from black to grey. He was reaching sixty when I met him. His suits were old but well tailored, his waistcoats or cardigans were stained; unkind people said that they didn't need cleaning so much as distilling, for he had a great liking for his native drink. He was an excellent diagnostician and despite his irregular visits his patients adored him. Some of the older ones would talk about his wife, who had deserted him and taken their only child, a daughter, back to Scotland, and his charwoman remembered him as 'a gradely looking chap, but a great big fool in marrying yon flighty piece'.

Once or twice he mentioned his daughter, Morag, to me. He seemed proud that she was a qualified doctor, working in a hospital over the border. Like any good Scot he was careful with his money, and invested his savings in property, and although he was never stuck for an excuse as to why he wasn't able to visit his patients, he'd never been known to miss a Friday night, driving round the streets in his battered old Morris, to collect his rents. He also owned a flourishing market garden in the nearby village of Fernlea. It was on his visits there that we nurses would meet him socially, for we used the local pub, The Mermaid, for our regular get-togethers. He would never join our table, possibly because he might have been persuaded into buying a round, but would converse with us by shouting from the bar. He was on friendly terms with all the regulars, but would never discuss medical matters with them. If anyone began talking about his aches and pains, he would get short shrift. 'Go and see yer ain doctor.' He did discuss vegetables, and would always be complaining at the low price they were fetching; he was worse than the most pessimistic of the farmers. After drinking a few double whiskys his hand would dive into his waistcoat pocket, he'd withdraw a large gold watch, check the time with the pub clock, and with a 'Yer bloody clock's still five minutes fast, don't ye think it's time ye poot it right' he'd make a quick exit.

The Laird lived in, and worked from, his house, The Priory. It was a large detached building, in what I suppose would be called a run-down part of the town. The other houses in the street were of the four-storied terraced type that years ago had housed prosperous middle-class families, but now were apartment houses where as many as four or five families lived in near squalor.

From the look of it outside, the Laird's house matched its fellows. The drive gate had rotted away from its hinges and had been thrown into the dirty privet bushes inside the garden wall; what had once been two pieces of lawn on either side of the broken tiled path, which led from the entrance pillars to the front door, had been roughly converted into a forecourt, with large, ugly, grey paving stones. The heavy brass plate bearing his name and qualifications, of which he must have once been so proud, was green through lack of cleaning, and almost unreadable. That of his partner, Doctor Pringle, had fallen away from its moorings on one side, and hung lopsidedly underneath its counterpart. During the day the heavy oak door was left open, showing a lobby with peeling yellow paint. The whole setting screamed of germs, though as you opened the door leading from the lobby into the long hall, you were assailed with such a pungent smell of Jeyes fluid that you wondered how man, or microbe, could live in such an atmosphere. It was rumoured that the doctor had an arrangement with the corporation drain-cleaners, whereby he swopped bottles of medicine for gallon cans of this disinfectant. If you arrived during the morning surgery, the doctor's cleaning woman would be mopping the tiles in the hall, and as you went in would scream, 'Don't put your feet on there, I've just mopped it down.' I once heard an elderly patient reply, 'If you think I'm going to walk on my hands with the pain I've got in my bloody back, you've got another think coming.'

The waiting room, which had been the drawing room of the house in bygone days, was furnished with many of the pieces the previous owners had left behind. These included a black leather window seat, a leather bolster-rolled couch and a quantity of black leather straight-backed chairs. Their broken springs caused suffering to some patients, and many were forced to stand, supporting themselves at the stained marble mantelpiece.

For the children it was a paradise, and they showed their appreciation of it by pulling tufts of horse hair from the tears in the leather, and scattering it around the room, and the 'Airs on a broken spring' that they played were demonstrations of their musical skills. Against one wall was a heavy mahogany table with carved legs, which was littered with tatty magazines. Although the war had been over for many years it seemed that it was the Laird's wish that patients should be reminded of unhappier days; perhaps he hoped that the pictures of blood and guts, and refugees herding across Europe, would make them realize that they were not half as badly off as they thought they were. Doctor Pringle added copies of *My Weekly* and *People's Friend* to these; they were his mother's and housekeeper's reading. One patient saw a recipe which she liked the sound of, and being an honest woman, took it with her into the surgery and asked Doctor Fairlie if she could borrow the magazine and copy it out. The Laird grunted and said, 'It would be much more satisfactory if ye gave me the price of the magazine, then ye can keep it.'

'Very well,' was the reply, 'if you'll tell me how much it cost, I'll make a cheque out for you here and now.'

He acknowledged defeat, 'All right, tak it, ye wily woman ye.'

The Laird's consulting room was opposite the waiting room, facing to the front of the house; Doctor Pringle's was further down the corridor, near the staircase. At the bottom of the stairs, on a table, stood a cage containing a mynah bird – Hamish. During his life, amongst the other expressions he'd picked up were a few medical ones, 'Put yer tongue out', 'Take a big breath', 'In out, in out'. Another favourite was, 'Bloody bad again, are yer?' and this caused considerable consternation to the newly-appointed headmaster of the local grammar school on his first visit. As he entered the hall he turned like a spinning top as the remark was squawked at him, before he discovered who the culprit was. Hamish must have had a sense of humour, for some days he would call, 'Next, please,' at regular intervals, and since no one was sure whether it was the Laird, Doctor Pringle, or the bird, the waiting room took on the appearance of a game of musical chairs, with people jumping up, going into the hall, bobbing back, and sitting down again.

Poor Doctor Pringle found the bird hard to live with, and was heard to say it was a hazard to his reputation as a doctor. 'Whenever I put a stethoscope to a patient's chest, the wretched thing squawks or whistles; I'm sure one day

I shall make a wrong diagnosis. The thing is a menace to medicine.'

His other colleagues at the doctors' club pretended sympathy. Doctor Jerry O'Dea, one of the younger ones, offered some practical advice.

'I know what you're going through,' he said, 'I've had a similar experience myself. When I was a houseman at a Birmingham hospital, I fell for the sweetest little student nurse. Unfortunately the hours she had to return to the nurses' home did not coincide with those of our affection, so I arranged with one of the maids there to leave a kitchen window open, through which I could heave my dear one when we were ready for her return. Everything seemed set fair for our romance, but we'd reckoned without the parrot. That bird, like Hamish, sat in its cage at the foot of the stairs, and when Molly, for that was my sweet girl's name, passed it on her way to bed at around two in the morning, it squawked "Good night, nurse" so loudly that the assistant matron awoke and caught Molly red-handed, as it were. It took me well over a week to persuade her to try again, for I thought it was a sort of one off, on the parrot's part. I was wrong, the same thing happened. Now I knew that the course of true love never did run smooth, but I didn't see why mine should be roughed up by a wretched parrot. So the following day I borrowed a chloroform spray, and gave the bird a squirt from it. I didn't mean to do it a permanent injury, but I thought a few days' sick leave wouldn't do it any harm. I was wrong.

I'd given it a swift, but painless, end. When I met Molly that same evening she told me the bird was dead. Like a fool, I explained that I was responsible. Instead of being proud at what I had done for her sake, she began crying, called me a heartless beast, said she'd never see me again and rushed out of my life. But you need have no such fears over Hamish. You would be acting in the cause of humanity, and I'm sure no one here would ever split on you.'

Either Doctor Pringle doubted the authenticity of Jerry O'Dea's story, feared that chloroform wouldn't do the trick, or was too soft-hearted, for the bird remained alive, continued to torment him, and to tease the patients.

The Laird's consulting room was of a similar size to the waiting room. Privacy was given in the daytime by a half window of net curtains, and in the evening by blackout drapes – another reminder of the war. The examination couch was against the wall which separated the room from the hall; the doctor's desk was in the bay window, with the swivel-chair facing the door, so that he was able to have a good look at patients as they made their way to the upright chair on the other side of the desk. The usual glass cupboard containing his instruments and equipment was in a recess at the side of his desk; in fact, except for a large grandfather clock which stood against the wall between the door and the handbasin, his consulting room looked little different from any other GP's. But time stood still in this room, for the hands of the clock always indicated that it was half-past-one, and no tick or chime issued from it. This perhaps was not surprising, for the bottom of the clock, when the door was open, displayed three large bottles. The one on the right contained a red-coloured mixture, the one on the left, a whiteish cloudy mixture, and the one in the middle, a clear brown liquid. I often noticed concoctions in red or whiteish bottles in the homes of the Laird's patients. The brown liquid I found was for the use of the doctor only, for many a time when I was reporting on one of his cases he would interrupt me by tapping his forefinger on the side of his nose, rising to his feet and journeying across the room. He would open the clock door, remove a tumbler from the shelf above the handbasin, half fill it from the centre bottle, take a quick gulp, shudder slightly, replenish his glass, replace the bottle and return to his desk. Then caressing the drink between his large hands would say, 'This, nurse, is the finest medicine in the whole world,' followed quickly by, 'Ah would like ye to join me in tasting it, but ah know ye lasses niver touch strong drink while on duty.' Then conscience cleared, he would take another mouthful, wipe his moustache with the back of his hand and lean forward and ask, 'Noo what were we saying?'

While it was obvious what the Laird's own medicine was, I was curious to know the contents of those other two bottles, for it seemed that he prescribed them for all ailments, from head to toe. The labels on the bottles gave nothing away, there was no pharmacist's name, they just read 'The Mixture. Take one dessert-spoonful, three times a day'. The first thing I found from my research was that if the red mixture didn't produce the desired effect, patients were given a bottle of the white, and vice versa. The next was that the majority of his patients swore by them, for when I questioned them, I was greeted with remarks like 'It's the greatest stuff ah've ever taken. Better than all them newfangled things young doctors give ye'; 'If it weren't for Doctor Fairlie's medicine, I'd have been kicking up the daisies long ago'; and even, 'It's cured my duodenal ulcer when nothing else would shift it.' When a middle-aged lady confided in me that her husband had been much more attentive since he'd been taking 'that red stuff', I decided to try it myself. 'Do you the world of good,' was the comment of the patient from whom I begged a teaspoonful. It tasted sweet and warm. Later that day I was able to sample the whiteish medicine. That also was sweet, and peppermint flavoured. It got me nowhere. I was now so intrigued with my research I decided to go round to the doctors' club, in the hope of seeing Doctor Pringle. He was just leaving as I arrived. I grabbed him by his coat tails, 'Doctor, there's something I've got to know, what does Doctor Fairlie put in those two medicines of his?' He roared with laughter. 'Come on in and have a drink, and I'll give you the recipes for those panaceas of all ills.' So it was that I discovered that the red contained just water, glucose and ginger, with cochineal to give it colour, and the white cloudy mixture, water, peppermint and bicarbonate of soda. When I protested at Doctor Fairlie's dishonesty, he quickly interrupted me, 'Now, nurse, you know even if it does no good, it can do no harm; you know too that Doctor Fairlie is a fine doctor, even if we do joke about him at times, and that his patients worship him. So if he does a bit of deception to separate the sheep from the goats, who's to blame him.'

I don't know whether it was the mynah bird that drove Doctor Pringle away, or the Laird's increasing habit of pushing his own cases over to him, but not long after I'd joined the service it was announced that Doctor Pringle had resigned from Doctor Fairlie's practice, and was joining forces with Doctor Rankin, another local practitioner. Then came the news that Doctor Morag Fairlie had filled the vacancy, and would be in partnership with her father. 'Now perhaps The Priory will get a face-lift,' was our immediate comment; but the Laird was too old for change, so a house was bought for his daughter near our nursing centre and was converted into what for Burrowdale was a modern masterpiece. The Laird could be seen daily talking to the workmen, and scratching his head in dismay as he watched his money pouring into 'this modern monstrosity', as he referred to it.

There was, of course, great speculation about Morag. She would be the first woman doctor Burrowdale had known; patients' reactions were not very complimentary, and strangely most of the criticism came from women.

We wondered too whom she would take after, her flighty mother, or the cunning, great big bear of a father.

We were all disappointed. She was tall, with the features of the Laird, but with none of his eccentric ways. She seemed determined to shun her own sex. Her black hair was pulled round under her ears and gathered in a severe bun at the back. She wore no make-up and underneath her white surgery coat were always Fair Isle sweaters and tweed skirts, no-nonsense lisle stockings and brogue shoes. She never smiled, and her only pleasure seemed to be in taking long country walks, moving in manly strides and carrying a knobkerrie. 'She's no need for that,' I heard someone comment, 'nobody's likely to assault her.' She took her work seriously, too seriously for some, as though it was a constant challenge. 'Busty' Clarke took against her on sight. 'Gives our sex a bad name.'

'If she'd been the opposite you'd still have disliked her,' I commented. 'Don't you remember saying that she'd probably be a Scottish Jezebel. No woman can win in your eyes.'

Morag had arrived early in December, and though Christmas could be just another working day for most of us, the Medical New Year's Ball at The Royal Hotel was an occasion when we expected to be able to put our work on one side, and to enjoy the evening without interruption. It was also the Laird's great night. He hired a Rolls Royce taxi, and, dressed in a colourful kilt and sporran and dragging a set of bagpipes at his side, would march into the hotel and head for the bar. It was the one night of the year that he managed to forget the value he attached to money; he bought drinks all round at least five times during the night. The bagpipes were surrendered into the care of the barman, with instructions that they were to be presented to him at five minutes to twelve, and on the stroke of midnight he would march round the room playing 'Auld Lang Syne', then lead the band in a series of lilting Scottish airs. When he took to the floor he danced like a dervish, any young nurse near at hand was grabbed into his arms and swung round like a puppet, and the following morning we would compare the bumps and bruises we'd sustained at his hands. Only Mrs Mac could discipline him, and the pair of them giving a performance of the Highland Fling was the highlight of the ball.

As the end of the year drew nearer, there was speculation among us as to how he would behave at the coming New Year's ball. Would the dour daughter's presence cast a shadow over the celebrations?

When I called at the nursing centre in the early afternoon before New Year's Eve, I was summoned by Evelyn Telford and told that I was required to attend a Mr Walter Tunstall, a patient of Morag Fairlie. I thought it was doubtful that I would find out how the dance went from first hand, for it seemed likely that my night would have to be spent on duty, though the assistant superintendent told me that everything possible would be done to see that I was relieved in time.

74

I knew old Walter Tunstall well. He had been one of the Laird's patients, and was just the kind he would have shifted on to his daughter when she joined him. I'd tried to nurse him on several occasions when nature had told him, through his collapsing in the street, that his heart was going to pack up one day soon if he didn't take care of himself. He'd been in hospital a number of times, but the moment he felt a little better, had discharged himself against all medical advice. When I first visited him he told me he'd got a 'Kodak' heart, on account of his having had 'rheumatismal' fever at the age of sixteen. Despite his odd way of putting it, he was right, rheumatic fever nearly always causes heart lesions. In fact, he was now suffering from auricular fibrillations, the rapid, irregular contractions of the auricle, which is a heart chamber. Normal contractions of the auricle are about seventy to eighty per minute; in Walter's case they had risen to between three hundred and four hundred. He had been prescribed digoxin 0.25 mg twice daily, to help strengthen his heartbeat, and slow down the conducting power of the nervous mechanism within it. But Walter was not one for taking drugs, nor it seemed did he care for me calling on him twice a day to administer them. He'd told me so, in forceful language, and the door would be barred to me until his next collapse.

I tried every way I knew to cajole him into accepting me, and at one time I seemed to have got him under control. He even allowed me to use the needle on him twice a week when the Laird prescribed Mersalyl injections, to increase the urinary output, and so get rid of excess fluids in his body. Not unnaturally, an important part of this treatment was to restrict his fluid intake, and it was this that caused yet another rift between Walter and myself. On three occasions I saw him staggering out of The Anglers Arms. I reprimanded him, and explained the business of fluid restriction to him. 'Yer a bluddy spy, that's what ye are, it's a free bluddy country, so ye can get out and stay out. Ah'm not having a young whipper-snapper like you telling me what I should or should not sup.' I didn't give up, and I succeeded in getting in once again, but only for four injections, then it seemed the shutters were up for good.

I tried recruiting the help of his next-door neighbour, a gossiping woman of around fifty, who lived in the flat opposite. 'Ah'll 'ave no more truck with 'im. Ah got the meals on wheels to call on 'im, 'e 'ad two dinners off 'em, then threw the next one in the good ladies' faces. 'e's dead wicked with the bairns, too; 'e chucks buckets of water over 'em. Not to speak of the language the old bugger uses.' I began to think I'd made a mistake in seeking her assistance, for every time I went along to try and make Walter see sense and open his door to me, she would come out and lend what she thought was her support, but which only made Walter's temper that much worse. I could visualize him on the other side of the door losing his breath and going purple and I dreaded the thought it could be one of my impotent calls that could administer the *coup de grace* to the poor old soul. But the neighbour did prove useful in one way. It was she who raised the alarm when she hadn't seen or heard anything of him for three or four days. She rang the police, who forced an entrance into his flat and found him in bed in a critical condition. They rang for the ambulance, but unfortunately, by the time it arrived, Walter had recovered sufficiently to tell the men that they could 'bugger off' because he was too ill to go into hospital. He refused to be moved, so the ambulance men got the name of his doctor from him, and Morag had been sent for.

When I drew up outside Walter's flat his neighbour was standing outside, talking to another woman.

'Oh, Glad,' she cried, 'it's the district nurse. 'allo nurse.' I returned her greeting. 'Come to see Walter, ah s'pose,' she went on. ''E's 'ad no end of visitors today, the p'lice, ambulance, and a lady doctor, she's been twice, she spoke to us, didn't she, Glad? Didn't know we 'ad lady doctors in Burrowdale.' She then glanced at the pile of linen in my arms, 'Ah see yer takin' things into 'im. That lady doctor took somethin' up, didn't she, Glad? Sheets, rugs and the like – oh and a bucket and mop; brand new it were, the price was still on it, wasn't it, Glad? No doctor ever bought me nowt, and ah've 'ad six kids. It seems the worse you be'ave the better you get treated, isn't that so, Glad?'

By the end of her *spiel* I was through the inside door and climbing the stairs; Walter's flat was on the first floor.

As I walked to his front door I was assailed by the smell of stale vomit, yet when I went into the sitting room it was clean and tidy and a refreshing smell of Savlon was doing its best to swamp all others. On a chair, by the sitting-room table, was a neat stack of clean sheets, pillow-cases, a blanket and two pairs of pyjamas. I moved into the bedroom. Walter lay on his old feather mattress, but I noticed the bed was covered with an expensive tartan car rug. He was breathing in short gasps, and his face, which was turned towards the window, was almost navy blue in colour. This room, like the sitting room, had been trans-formed from its usual filthy and untidy self; the tops of the window sill and the chest of drawers had been cleared, and on a chair by his bed were his pipe and tobacco pouch, his old pocket watch, a few silver and copper coins and ironically, an empty beer bottle against which was propped a letter addressed to 'The District Nurse'. I opened it; it was written in Morag's typical doctor's scrawl, so I had some difficulty reading it. It stated that all four chambers of Walter's heart were pumping independently (normally they pump in unison), that his heart muscle was grossly enlarged, that there was no chance of a recovery, and it was now only simply a matter of ensuring that he was kept comfortable. She'd also written that she'd given him an injection of Lasix, another diuretic drug; she apologized for it being likely, therefore, that his bed would be wet, but that in the sitting room I would find some fresh bed linen and pyjamas. She ended by saying that since Walter had expressed the wish to remain at home, we must respect this and do our best to see that his last hours were as easy as we could make them.

I went close to the bed. I could see that Walter was moribund, but I knew that if he was still conscious I would have to move carefully.

'Hallo, Mr Tunstall,' I began. 'Not feeling so good, eh?'

His head moved slightly as he tried to focus his glazed eyes on me, then he whispered, 'What are you going to do to me?'

'I'm here to make you comfortable, don't worry, there'll be no needles this time.'

He sighed, as though satisfied at what I'd said. I put my hand under the covers and as Morag had prophesied the bed was very wet, but there were two hot-water bottles there so his skin felt quite warm.

I went through the sitting room and into the small kitchen. It was as dirty as usual. I filled the black kettle and lit the stove. There was a horrible smell of gas, for since the jet was so filthy it only partly came alight. Under the sink I found a cracked enamel basin, and then I saw the new bucket and mop, which were the envy of Walter's neighbours. 'Walter,' I thought to myself, 'I know you're close to the angels, but it seems to me that you've already met one in Morag Fairlie.' For never in my nursing career had I known a doctor to clean and mop up rooms, let alone buy the utensils to do it with, and as if that wasn't enough, to bring fresh linen and an expensive car rug to a grumpy old soul who had always made life so difficult for the people who had been anxious to help him.

When I returned to his bedroom with the basin of hot water, I went up and whispered, 'God's on your side, Walter.' I hadn't been able to find any towels or face cloths, so I tore one of the sheets I'd brought into sizes to serve the purpose. Giving Walter what is termed 'General Nursing Care' was a long process, needing many kettles of hot water. Each time I moved a limb he seemed to stop breathing. I would then check his radial pulse, which would almost fade out, return in weak volume, and increase to a rapid and irregular rate. When I turned him on his side, so that I could roll the clean sheet, the mackintosh sheet and draw sheet under him, he offered no resistance and when I went round to the other side, where his body now lay, I was almost certain that he was dead. I picked up a very limp arm and again felt for his pulse; it was still coming through feebly and erratically. I kicked off my shoes, climbed on to the bed, and moved Walter over to the other side, got down again and hurriedly pulled the sheets through. I then put the back rest I'd brought in place and laid four pillows across it. Again I had to climb on to the bed and lift him to a sitting position. This done, I changed his pyjama jacket, deciding against the trousers, as I felt the effort of putting his legs into them would prove too much for his already exhausted heart.

I then stood back to survey my handiwork. Walter's face was still a deep shade of blue and he was breathing in shallow and rapid gasps, but at least he no longer had that dirty neglected appearance, and seeing him lying there in his clean pyjama jacket, between white sheets, head resting comfortably on the pillows, with his bed covered in a tartan car rug, I felt quite proud of my achievements. One last touch was needed. I looked around for a comb, but finding none took mine from my handbag, and passing it through his scanty remnants managed to leave him with a neat quiff across his forehead. I decided that perhaps I had no further use for the comb, and left it on the chair beside his bed. I leaned across, bent my face down to the level of his ear, and said, 'How do you feel now, Walter?' His eyes opened and as he tried to speak I noticed that his tongue needed cleaning, but from the feeble jerk that he gave when I tried to open his lips further I realized that he'd had enough for one session, so I settled for giving him a sip of water. It was what he wanted. He tried to get his arm up to grasp the cup, but couldn't make it. I held it to his mouth and as I did so I think I glimpsed the first look of gratitude in his tired old eyes.

It took me ten minutes to write my nursing report; I put it against the empty beer bottle on the chair near Walter's bed. I glanced at him once more, and thought that it seemed criminal to leave him lying there alone. Again I bent over him. 'Don't worry, someone will be here soon,' I murmured. His lips moved but no sound came from them. When I stepped outside his flat, there on the landing was the neighbour and 'Glad'. 'Hi, nurse, 'ow's Walt?' she said harshly. For a moment I thought of asking one of them to go and sit with the dying man, but decided against it. The sight of a sworn enemy might well have been the end of him, so with a 'Not so good really' I walked down the stone steps and into my car. I drove to the nearest telephone kiosk and eventually spoke to Evelyn Telford. She told me to leave everything to her, that she would arrange for a 'night sitter', that she would also visit Walter herself, and that I was now to continue with my other visits.

I was late for the Hogmanay Ball, and so was Evelyn Telford. More conspicuous by his absence was the Laird. He'd always been one of the first arrivals, so there was a deal of speculation as to what had happened to him. I'm afraid most people blamed his daughter. 'She's probably kept him at home. She's not one for parties herself, so she's spoiling his fun. He's not been the same man since she's been here,' were the kind of remarks that were bandied around. I kept my counsel. I wasn't ready yet to report on the new Morag that I had discovered that day.

When it came to half-past-ten I think most of us were resigned to the fact that the Laird would not be with us, and we set about having as good an evening as possible without him. It was only minutes later that a wail of bagpipes came from the hotel foyer, and as it grew nearer and mingled with the music of the band, the sound was fearsome. The doors were flung open, the band stopped, giving the pipes pride of place, and we all applauded the two figures as they marched in. Our enthusiasm wasn't just for the familiar figure of the Laird; it was as much for a transformed Morag. She looked radiant. Her shining hair was coiled round her head and held there by a simple band of pearls. Over her shoulder was thrown a plaid caught on one side by a silver double-hearted brooch. Under this plaid showed a white blouse with a lace jabot. Her long tartan skirt hung to the floor and two silver-buckled shoes peeped from under the hem. As they stepped on to the ballroom floor she left her father's side, and catching her skirt in her left hand, broke into a lilting Scottish dance, with the Laird taking up his cue, puffing away on the bagpipes. We all joined in with the wild cries that seemed so much part of the music, and we clapped in time with the tune. When it ended she rushed to the bar and it was drinks all round on Morag.

Everyone agreed it was her evening, even the Laird gave her pride of place and contented himself basking in her glory, and reserving the slow waltzes to lead her on to the floor. He played the New Year in on the pipes, and afterwards we all called for another performance from Morag. I think it was generally felt that it was the finest party in the memory of anyone present, and there were many people biting their tongues at their earlier criticism of Doctor Morag Fairlie. Colin and I decided to walk home and on the way we talked of the two sides I had seen of this splendid woman during the last twenty-four hours.

It was work as usual the following day, and at nine o'clock I drew up once more at Walter's flat. Again the neighbours were there to greet me, "'Allo, nurse, that lady doctor's up yon. Bin there since three in the mornin', she 'as.' I began wondering when she slept. 'She must 'ave walked for 'er car's not 'ere. Now why do yer think she did that?'

'I've no idea,' I said flatly, as I made my way upstairs.

When I went into Walter's bedroom, Morag was bending over him, sounding his chest with her stethoscope. Her black hair was swept back in its familiar bun, her silver buckled shoes were replaced by the heavy brown brogues, and she was wearing a shapeless tweed coat. As she straightened up and removed the stethoscope she looked at me professionally and unemotionally. 'Good morning, nurse, I'm afraid this unfortunate gentleman is now comatosed.' I raised the bed covers, found the sheets wet; although the bottles were still hot, Walter's skin was cold and clammy. His mouth was open, and the short rapid gasps of yesterday had changed to noisy stertorous spasmodic sighs. I felt that the slightest movement of his body would extinguish the faint flames of life still flickering within it. Nevertheless I asked Doctor Morag if I should change the wet draw sheet. With eyes on his distorted features, she shook her head.

We stood, one on each side of the bed, for almost half an hour, without exchanging a word, each taking turns to damp the blue lips with water. The pauses between the long sighs lengthened, and eventually ceased. We waited, listening for another feeble sigh, but only a weak gurgling sound came from the back of Walter's throat, then his head lolled down on his right shoulder, and I sent up a prayer to whoever was in charge of the gates of heaven, in the hope that they would treat him leniently and let him enter.

Morag moved to check his chest sounds with her stethoscope: there were none. I removed the back rest and pillows and gently laid his head on the mattress, then closed the partially open eyes; the doctor pulled the top covering sheet over his face. Morag broke the long silence as we walked out of the bedroom, 'Can you give me a lift home, nurse?' On the landing stood the now familiar figure of the neighbour. She didn't speak, our expressions must have given the answer to the question that was on her lips. During the short car journey I said that I would inform Evelyn Telford of the death, and that through her arrangements would be made for the funeral. There were six of us present at the service, Morag, myself, some relation of Walter's and his wife, his neighbour and her friend Glad. The last two cried throughout the service, whether from some last-minute affection or from remorse at the way they had treated him during his last years, it was impossible to know.

Another more important mystery to me in this case was Doctor Morag's behaviour. She had appointed herself as guardian angel to a grumpy, alcoholic, ne'er-do-well. She had shown devotion far beyond the call of duty. Why? There was nothing she could prove to herself or the world by her actions. Many indeed would say that no doctor should use time on a hopeless case, where death was inevitable, possibly even desirable. My interpretation of it was this: that those of us who have elected to tend the sick have from time to time to remind ourselves exactly what this means, and in the fullest possible terms. This then was why Walter's last hours were spent with as much dignity and care as could be given to him.

Chapter Five

Heathfield Hall, like our nurses' home, had been a large Victorian house before it had been converted into a private hotel. Between the wars, when times were hard in Burrowdale, it was bought by a group of doctors in the town, and easily lent itself to a further conversion into a club, the Medics Club, as we called it. It was close to the nurses' centre and although we couldn't become members there was always someone to welcome us as guests. Sometimes, if we wanted to discuss patients, it was easier to pop into the club to see the doctor concerned, rather than try to get him on the phone or at his surgery; it was also more friendly. It was very much like any social club, with a bar, dining and sitting rooms, and card and billiard rooms. Apart from exchanging information about patients we were also able to get to know something of the private lives of the men whose instructions so largely affected our own working lives.

I've always felt sorry for doctors' wives (my husband Colin tells me he has often felt sorry for himself!), for although they share many of the disadvantages of their husbands' work – perpetual telephone calls, message-taking and disturbed nights – they are rewarded by a patronizing anonymity. 'This is Doctor So and So's wife.' At Heathfield Hall, however, the wives came into their own, indeed they often seemed to take over, and many a doctor must at times have wished the club had been restricted to men only.

Doctor Henry Rankin was perhaps the most distinguished of all the medical men in Burrowdale. He was very professional, his instructions were always given in clear-cut tones, and with an exact and concise account of the patient's symptoms and a history of illnesses. When he gave orders he expected them to be carried out to the letter, and woe betide any nurse who, thinking she knew better, changed his prescribed treatment. When angry he spoke in a clipped voice, and this and his cold logic cut through any attempted defence. His nickname, one which he'd been christened by his junior partner, Ashley Cruickshank, was 'The Big Fella', and since Doctor Cruickshank was several inches taller than his partner, he obviously wasn't referring to his physical stature.

If, as is said, behind every successful man is an astonished wife, then Mrs Emily Rankin gave truth to the saying. She did everything she knew how to belittle her husband, with interruptions like, 'No, Henry, you haven't got that quite right'; 'I'm afraid Henry's getting a little forgetful in his old age'; 'Henry, I'm sure you've told that story a hundred times before, and everyone is getting very bored with hearing it'. At other times she would attack his appearance, 'Henry, I've told you so many times, you shouldn't be wearing that tie, it was designed for a much younger man', and there were frequent references made to his balding head. I longed for the day when his lips would narrow, and his clipped voice would destroy her, but it never came. Instead he would break into a tolerant smile, and with his 'Yes, my dear' would turn the other cheek.

There were other ways Emily Rankin made her presence felt, for she was an organizer. Now I don't want to give offence to the many women who work for charities, I applaud their efforts, and in my own way I have, I think, done my bit in my time, but there are ways of organizing, and Mrs Rankin's didn't suit me, or indeed any of my colleagues. She would rush into the club bar in her coat and hat, as if she'd no intention of staying, click her fingers at Henry from the doorway as an instruction for him to order her a sweet martini, and then begin attacking the occupants of the nearest table: 'We're organizing a coffee morning/sherry evening/cheese and wine party/cider and sausage party/punch and pâté party, may I put your name down? I know you'll enjoy it, there'll be such a nice class of people there, and we hope our Member will be coming.'

'Whose Member?' 'Busty' Clarke asked sweetly one day, which took some of the wind out of Emily's sails. If ever Emily succeeded in bludgeoning a nurse into attending one of these functions, she was immediately enlisted to do much of the work. 'How good of you, dear; now I know I can call on your assistance. If you can be with us an hour before, then you can help get things ready and you won't mind handing round for us, will you? And if you can bring along a few things like sandwiches, sausage rolls or cakes. Thank you, I knew I could rely on you.' It was no use saying that we were on call at that particular time. 'What a pity,' would be the reply, 'but I'm sure you've got a friend who would like to come along,' and an invitation would be thrust into your hand, and a half crown expected in hers. 'Busty' reached her ultimate in rudeness once when she had this offer of one for a friend: 'Mrs Rankin, I've given away four of your invitations, and now I haven't got any friends.' Since there was no comeback to this, Emily tossed her head in the air, and sniffed, 'Really, Nurse Clarke, I'm sure I've given no cause for such an ill-mannered remark.'

Fortunately we soon learned that Emily worked to a pattern. She moved methodically down the tables, first one side and then the other. Her work completed she would then again click her fingers, which was a signal for Henry to finish his drink and return home with her. As this regular pattern of Emily's movements became apparent, we would either change sides, or drink up quickly and leave before she reached us.

Emily's behaviour was something that 'Busty' Clarke and Evelyn Telford were in absolute agreement over. One day, Mrs Rankin called at the nursing centre with some books of raffle tickets, and asked the assistant superintendent if she would distribute them around the district nurses. 'I'm sure all their patients would be happy to buy some tickets,' she said. It was a grave error of judgement.

'Mrs Rankin,' replied Evelyn, 'I'm sure my nurses' patients would buy them, they would feel morally bound to, but it's a kind of blackmail that neither I, nor my staff, would tolerate.'

Brenda Cruickshank, as the junior partner's wife, was, inevitably, frequently involved. It was an open secret that she deliberately got pregnant so as to make a dignified escape, and when her baby was born someone was heard to remark to her, 'What are you going to call him, Raffles?'

The Medics Club was also useful to me as a bank. Often I was unable to find the time to cash a cheque, and if I needed money, Bob the barman would oblige. One evening, when I walked into the bar for that purpose, I was hailed by Doctor Rankin, 'Just the person I want to see.' He glanced over his shoulder, I felt, to make sure his wife hadn't come in. 'Let me buy you a drink; then, if you don't mind, we'll go into the card room and we can have a talk; there'll be no one in there at the moment.' We made our way across the hall and sat at a table.

'Nurse, have you ever heard of someone being killed by kindness?'

I was astonished by his question, and replied rather lamely that, though I'd heard the expression, I'd never had a case that I could put in that category.

'Well, if I can persuade you to take it on, you're going to have one now. You know George Street?'

'Indeed I do,' I replied. Indeed I did. It was part of an Edwardian housing estate on the outskirts of town; the other part was Edward Street. The two backed on to each other and formed what was known as The Village. It was like a village; it was as though at some time the community had decided to break away from the rest of the town and become self-supporting. Some of the houses had been turned into shops and there were allotments and smallholdings nearby, where vegetables, eggs, poultry, even home-cured bacon and pork (for many people kept their own pigs) could be bought; so it came about that a visit into Burrowdale for the villagers was a rare occasion. The other nurses called it 'Pat's village', for there were few houses that at one time or another I hadn't visited, and when I walked down either street the greetings I got from the residents would have been the envy of royalty. But to return to Doctor Rankin. 'Then if you know George Street you may know the Greenhoughs.' To my surprise I didn't. My mind did a quick race up and down the street, but I couldn't place them, and I said so. 'They live in one of the new houses at the top end,' he explained. That was why I hadn't heard of them, though I knew something of the history of the houses. To the annoyance of the villagers, a market gardener had obtained planning permission to build six semi-detached homes, which appealed to what might be called a better class of purchaser, but these people didn't appeal to the villagers, who had their own particular type of apartheid.

'Anyway,' the doctor went on, 'the Greenhoughs were patients of mine long before they moved to George Street, and so have stayed on my panel. They have one child, Amanda, who's now ten years old and this is the poor little creature that, as I said earlier, is being killed by kindness. I'll tell you her case history.

'I first met Amanda when she was three. Her mother and father brought her to me because she was still incontinent. I noticed that she was walking unsteadily and after I'd examined her I felt sure she had a spinal deformity, and advised a consultation with an orthopaedic surgeon. Mr Greenhough then hit the roof. "We brought our daughter to see if you could advise us on her incontinence, now you seem to be making out she's some sort of freak." I tried explaining that her possible deformity didn't make her a freak, and that the two things were probably closely allied, but he would have none of it and left the surgery in a huff. I heard nothing more of them for four years, then I had a visit from the school medical doctor, who confirming my original diagnosis had run into similar trouble with her father, which the doctor had made worse by stating categorically that the girl should be sent to a school for physically handicapped children. Again there was nothing we could do. I wrote to the parents, suggesting that they might like to come and see me, but they didn't reply to my letter. Two more years passed, then an abashed and very penitent Mrs Greenhough telephoned me, asking for an appointment. This time I got tough and said there was no point in them coming to see me, if they were not prepared to act on my advice. Mrs Greenhough admitted that circumstances had shown they were wrong, and that both she and her husband were willing to put the child completely in my hands.

'When we met I discovered that it was the treatment that Amanda had received from the children at school that had forced her parents to change their minds. Her incontinence had made her the laughing stock of the class, and of course their taunts had aggravated her condition. Physically she had developed slowly and was very small for her age. I sent them to see Doctor Walker at Preston, who in his turn sent them to a consultant orthopaedic surgeon at one of the London teaching hospitals, and on his instruction Amanda was operated on in two stages, both successfully, and after six months returned home.' Doctor Rankin paused for a moment, then he smiled, almost wryly, 'Now I come to the tricky part of the story. It's where the biter got bitten. I had remonstrated with them before for not giving their child the attention she needed, now she was getting it in full measure; it seemed the mother's whole world revolved round her. That might have been all right for a time, if Amanda hadn't seized control of the revolving. She'd obviously enjoyed being a patient and an invalid, and her mama had enjoyed, as it were, a baby in her care again; father was now the wretched ogre, who hadn't wanted Amanda to be treated properly. Briefly, nurse, Amanda now refuses to go to the physiotherapist – she can hardly walk at all, so she no longer goes to school and her incontinence, from which she'd almost recovered while she was in hospital, has returned. I think unconsciously I've created a situation which I'm unable to resolve. I believe you can. Will you try?'

I began by saying that I felt he really couldn't blame himself for the outcome, at which he roared with laughter, 'Don't worry, nurse, I'm not becoming a psychological mess as a result of it.' Then he became serious again, 'But I'm very concerned, and I promise you that if you take on the case, I'll give you all the help in my power.'

'Of course I'll do it,' I replied, 'but you'll have to clear it with Mrs Telford first.'

'I'm afraid I've already taken the liberty of doing that,' he smiled. 'I understand you begin tomorrow morning. Good luck, and thank you.'

As he left, I swore, 'Bloody men', at that time the nearest we got to the expression 'male chauvinist pigs'.

The Greenhoughs' home was third in the row of new semi-detached houses. As I slowly drove up George Street, I was conscious of the movement of curtains in many of the front rooms on either side of the road, and in my car mirror I could see that the more inquisitive had come outside, and were leaning against their front doors to discover which house I was going to. I didn't resent their curiosity; in nearly every instance it would, I knew, be out of good neighbourliness, for if anyone was sick in George Street, there was no shortage of people to help in every possible way and I was always quick to call on their kindness and generosity if a patient was in need. I could almost sense their feelings of disgust when I stopped outside the new houses. 'What right have they got to call our district nurse in?' they'd be saying and it would be the talking point of the gossip of the day.

The house was typical of its kind, with wrought-iron gates, bow window, glass-fronted door, and a ding-dong doorbell. The front garden had a pocket handkerchief lawn and the plants were arranged with the regularity of soldiers. The door was opened by a pretty chocolate-boxy kind of woman, in her early thirties. She gushed, 'Oh, nurse, how good of you to call; dear Doctor Rankin told me to expect you. Please come in, mind the step, let me take your coat. You'll have a cup of coffee, won't you?' Her 'Mandy will be thrilled to meet you, won't you, Mandy dear?' thrown a little louder than her other remarks fell on deaf ears. 'Do come into the lounge and we'll have a little chat. I shan't be a minute, I'll just go and get the coffee ready.'

I sat down in an easy chair, feeling mentally dishevelled. While Mrs Greenhough busied herself in the kitchen, I took stock of the surroundings. They matched the outside of the house; a place for everything, and everything in its place. There was a three-piece suite, floral-patterned carpet, striped wallpaper with matching curtains, an electric imitation coal fire in a beige-tiled grate, some seascape pictures around the walls and the inevitable three china ducks flying up it. Now I know the artist Peter Scott has done a lot for the preservation and conservation of the countryside, and its bird and animal life, but he carries a heavy responsibility for the disfigurement of countless sitting rooms in this country – those wretched painted ducks were everywhere, and they screamed at me from the walls of most of the houses that I entered; it got so that I even loathed the living creatures. But back to the Greenhoughs' sitting room: against the wall, opposite the fireplace, was a piano, open and with a sheet of music on its stand, in the bay window a chaise longue and a small cane-woven commode, partially shielded by a screen.

Mrs Greenhough entered with the coffee and a few biscuits.

'My name's Isobel. I think Christian names are so much more friendly, don't you, nurse?'

I agreed, without telling her mine; for the moment I wanted to preserve a professional relationship.

'I suppose I had better tell you Mandy's story from the beginning.'

I again agreed. It would be interesting, I thought, to compare her tale with Doctor Rankin's. It differed in detail, and was more personal, of course. It seemed she was laying most of the blame on her husband's attitude. She told me how she had stayed in London during the period Mandy was in hospital there, and seemed to imply that her husband, Tom, should have been with her.

'You won't repeat this, I know, nurse, but since Mandy's

operation Tom seems to ignore the poor little mite, it's as though he can't bear to look at her. He seemed to think that after the operation Mandy would be able to walk again almost immediately. Mind you, I think the hospital were to blame in raising his hopes as they did. Of course the staff there, although they were terribly kind, and I wouldn't want you to think I'm not grateful to them, didn't understand how timid and sensitive our dear little Mandy is. Well, they can't be expected to, can they, having so many patients to deal with, and nothing can replace a mother's love and care, can it?'

I suppose I must have made some sort of noise in reply. As she gave her story, I got more and more depressed.

'How is Mandy's walking now?' I asked.

'Not very good, I'm afraid.'

'But surely when she left the hospital she was getting on quite well.'

'Yes, she was,' came the reluctant reply. 'But I'm afraid Tom's attitude hasn't helped, he thought she would start walking directly she was back home, when I knew all she wanted was love and affection, after those weeks in hospital. Tom's mother doesn't help, either; I suppose it's natural that she should side with him, but I feel so terribly alone. Oh, nurse, I do hope you will understand and help me.'

I could see that tears were soon likely to follow, and I didn't want to be introduced to Mandy by a crying mother.

'I wonder if I could see Mandy now?'

'Yes, of course,' Isobel brightened. Then her face changed, 'But you will be gentle with her, won't you?'

I felt like saying that I would probably eat her, but contented myself with an 'Of course'.

Mandy was brought in in her mother's arms dressed as though she was going to a party, in a pink silk frock over frilly lace knickers, her hair in two neat plaits tied with pink satin ribbon. She'd little white socks and pink buttoned shoes, and round her neck was a gold chain with a heart-shaped locket. I almost laughed, then more charitably thought perhaps Isobel had dressed her like that specially for our first meeting; subsequent visits proved me wrong – at any rate for a time.

'Mandy, this is the nice nurse who's come to visit you and help you to walk properly again.'

'Hallo, Mandy,' I ventured, matter-of-factly. She buried her head in her mother's bosom. Isobel put her into a chair, and I tried another tack. 'Do you play the piano, Mandy?' I asked. The stupid Isobel pounced in, 'Yes, and she's very good for her age, aren't you, dear?' I tried again.

'What games do you like playing?'

'She's very fond of her dollies, aren't you, Mandy? Would you like me to fetch them and show nurse?'

'I want to go to the toilet.' At last she'd spoken, even though she'd said nothing constructive. Isobel rushed over to pick her up. 'Why don't you try letting her walk?' I suggested. It was a mistake, and Mandy proved it by wetting the chair, and the floor. I thought I'd done enough damage for one visit. I left while the mopping-up operation was still in progress.

I drove away in a state of depression. It was I supposed the most unsuccessful visit I'd ever had. It was not made any better when I rang Doctor Rankin and reported how disastrous it had been, and how I thought it was unlikely that I was ever going to get anywhere, for he replied, 'Don't worry, nurse, Rome wasn't built in a day.' It was, I thought, the most footling remark that he could have made under the circumstances.

I was down to visit Mandy twice a week, and between my first and second call I gave the case a lot of thought. It was obvious the first thing that was necessary was some-how for me to get the child's confidence and, if possible, her affection. It wasn't going to be easy because from what I'd seen of her so far she was everything I disliked most in children. I knew I would get no help from Isobel, who was feeding on her daughter's love, and was therefore jealously possessive. I could try to see Mr Greenhough privately, but that could be dangerous. It didn't require great powers of detection to see that the marriage was already in danger, and that if I appeared to be siding with one or the other the powder keg would explode, my position would become untenable and I would have done more harm than good. Then I wondered about the older Mrs Greenhough; it occurred to me that she might be a useful ally, though from what Isobel had said she was already suspect in her eyes.

As luck would have it, on my next visit she was there – by design I later found out – and she was everything I hoped she might be: a no-nonsense, down-to-earth kind of woman. She, Isobel and I had a chat while we drank coffee, and then, with what I hoped was a meaningful look at the grandmother, I said that I wanted to see Mandy and that I wished to be alone with her.

I don't think I've ever worked so hard to gain a patient's confidence. Mandy did nothing to help, nor could I use the kind of arguments that had almost become second nature to me when cajoling adults. By the end of my time with her, though, I'd persuaded her to walk for me. I thought of demonstrating this first show of confidence to the two ladies, but quickly changed my mind. 'We'll keep it a secret between us, Mandy; you work hard while I'm not here and one day, when you're ready, we'll show mummy how clever you've been.' She seemed excited about this, and promised to do her exercises and to practise walking. I told Isobel that Mandy and I had been getting to know each other, and left it at that. As I was about to go, the elder Mrs Greenhough asked if I would give her a lift. We'd just left 'The Village' when she suggested that I stopped the car so that we could talk. She then asked point-blank what my opinion was of the situation. I told her the way I saw it, leaving out my conjectures about the state of the marriage. 'You seem to see the situation very clearly, nurse, but before we talk about the best ways of putting it right, there's something else you should know: their marriage is in very great danger.' I then replied that I thought this might be the case.

'I believe it's probably worse than you think,' she went on. 'Tom is spending much more time with my husband and me. Normally we would be glad to see him, but not in his present state, he's drinking too much and it's obvious that he feels very bitter about everything. He hasn't spoken about leaving Isobel yet, but if things go on as they are doing, I'm sure it's only a matter of time, and very little time at that.'

I thought for a moment; it looked as if this Greenhough case showed nothing but unrelieved gloom and foreboding. There was one thing to be said for it: anything was worth trying, for if it failed the situation couldn't get much worse. Between us we worked something out. I would increase my visits to one a day and would try and get Mandy walking, so that we could show her progress to her mother as quickly as possible, while for their part, Tom's parents would sing Isobel's praises for what they would pretend she was doing for the child.

'If we can make it look as though she's been largely responsible for Mandy's recovery, I'm sure it will go a long way to bringing Isobel and Tom closer together again,' Mrs Greenhough said.

'You're assuming, of course, that we can get Mandy to recover,' I replied gloomily.

'Oh, I'm sure you'll be able to do that.'

I must say I wished people wouldn't show a confidence in me that I was far from feeling myself.

Yet things did begin to happen. Daily Mandy became more delighted with our plot, and it was only a fortnight before I felt we were able to give our exhibition to Isobel. During that time Mrs Greenhough senior kept well out of the way but 'she happened to be passing' when the moment arrived. Mandy excelled herself, and Mrs Greenhough and I mirrored her delight as without assistance she moved easily round the room. Not so Isobel, she looked on stonily, and when it was over held out her arms and said, 'Come to mummy, my poor darling, you must be tired out.'

'You bitch,' I nearly screamed, and as I looked at the other Mrs Greenhough I could see that she too was biting her lip to control herself.

'What now?' I asked her, when we left together. 'We're back at square one; heaven knows what that poor child's feelings are.'

'There seems to be only one chance left, and that's Tom,' she replied.

I couldn't see what he could do to help, and said so.

'You must persuade Mandy to give the same demonstration to her father on Saturday morning, and leave the rest to me,' was her non-committal answer.

I'd two days to do it in. I managed but it wasn't easy, as Mandy's confidence had been badly bruised. I didn't think she gave as good a performance as at our first demonstration, but Tom was tremendously impressed. 'Thank you, nurse, it's wonderful the progress that she's made,' and his eyes showed his delight.

I picked up my cue. 'You mustn't just thank me, it's Isobel who has given Mandy her confidence back,' I lied disarmingly.

He turned to his wife and put his arm round her shoulder, 'Darling, you've done it. I'm sorry, I never thought you could, please forgive me, I've been of so little help.' This, it seemed, was just what Isobel had been waiting for – the affection, that in recent months she had tried to replace through her daughter. I looked at Tom's mother.

'Nurse,' she said, 'I'm sorry to bother you but I must catch the shops before they close, so if I can cadge a lift . . .'

We were out of the house in a matter of seconds. I drove a few hundred yards, then stopped, and together we howled with delight. Our final ploy had worked. 'I'm not a regular drinker,' said Mrs Greenhough, 'but this calls for a celebration,' and we drove to her home and toasted each other over gin and tonics.

From then on Mandy's case was plain sailing. The headmaster of the school for physically handicapped children allowed a young teacher to provide Mandy with the further help she required, and it wasn't long before she was enrolled into the school. I had by then given up my regular visits, but I had made two other firm friends in George Street, Isobel and Tom Greenhough, who were now as close as a newly-married couple. Two months later

I was invited to go with them and Tom's mother to the swimming baths, where I stood and watched Mandy swim a length, and when we went home for tea afterwards I noticed that the divan and commode had been removed from the sitting room. What must in a way read like a fairy tale continued to unfold. Mandy eventually left her special school, went to a secondary modern, from there to a training college, and ended up teaching in a school for physically handicapped children. The family are now also part of 'The Village', and Mandy is always on call to play the piano at any of their parties or functions.

Doctor Rankin had followed the case through my brief written reports. He had not been disinterested, but was prepared to leave it in my hands, knowing that if I needed help I would ask for it. About two weeks after I had officially signed off, we met again in the doctors' club.

'I understand you had a success with the Greenhoughs,' he said. 'I'm most grateful to you, nurse; it must have taken a lot of your time.'

'Thank you, doctor,' I was quick to reply, 'it did. Rome wasn't built in a day, you know.'

Chapter Six

During the time I was working on Mandy's case, I became involved with another family. One winter's morning, I noticed a new name had been added to my work list – Gary Caine, aged six years, bronchial pneumonia, Crystamycin injections twice daily. Doctor Fairlie's patient. Address, 104 Wharf Street.

Wharf Street was a cobbled road leading from the docks. Though it was narrow, the houses on both sides were tall, early Victorian buildings, so that even on the finest day it seemed dark and dismal. What had once been family homes were now either apartment blocks, occupied by as many as four families, basement to attic, or warehouses; while some which had been left empty were well and truly vandalized. As the street straggled up the hill towards the centre of the town it improved somewhat, but never could it be classed as other than insalubrious. It was an area I didn't know very well, so before beginning my round I asked Sally Shaw, the oldest of my colleagues who knew Burrowdale like the back of her hand, where No. 104 lay. Never the friendliest of people, she scowled at me over the top of her bifocals, 'You should know that by now, No. 112 is the sweet shop on the corner of Wharf Street and Battenbury Row, so 104 must be on the dock side of that. Who've you got there anyway?' I showed her my work book. 'Never heard of anybody called Caine down there, must be the child of a rooming tenant, probably a whore; if so, the best of luck to you.'

As she sniffed her way off, the name started to ring a bell. Pearl Caine, Gary Caine six years old, my first delivery as a district midwife in Burrowdale, or, as I'd always thought of him, my rexine sofa baby. My curiosity now got the better of my repugnance at having to visit Wharf Street. I'd often wondered what had happened to Pearl, and it was always exciting for me to see how a baby I'd delivered had developed; though the diagnosis of bronchial pneumonia didn't promise well.

I got through my first calls – three insulin injections for diabetic patients – speedily, then headed for Wharf Street.

Number 104 was even worse than I'd expected. It stood between two vandalized, derelict houses, there were four steps up to the front door and on one side the protective iron railings hung drunkenly over the well of the basement. The door was ajar, so I pushed my way into the hall. Dark brown paintwork and filthy wallpaper were peeling off damp walls and a smell of human sweat, degradation and decay stifled the nostrils and coated the throat. There was no indication of who lived where, so for a moment I was at a loss as to what to do. I knew better than to open one of the doors leading from the passage, since anyone doing so at any time of the day or night was likely to get a glimpse of 'what the butler saw', and the language that followed on such an intrusion could be fearful. I decided therefore to alert one of the occupants of the house in the only possible safe way, by shouting: 'Hallo, is anyone at home?'

A door opened at the far end of the passage and two huge flaccid breasts bulging from a dirty pink negligée, and topped with a plastic white powder-coated face with hennaed hair, peered round it. A cigarette dangled from her lips, the smoke curling into her eyes narrowed them into a squint.

'Oo are you?' she demanded.

'The district nurse,' I replied, glancing down at my uniform.

'Watcher want?'

'I've called to see Gary Caine. I understand he's unwell.'

'You'll pass,' she said, as though she was a kind of sentry. 'Pearl and 'im are on the next floor up. They're abuv 'ere. Tell 'er I 'opes Gary ain't too bad.'

I followed her directions, conscious as I climbed the linoleum-covered stairs that she was watching me all the way, and I heard her door slam as I reached Pearl's.

She greeted me like a long-lost friend, 'Hi yer, nurse, well, ain't it grand, 'aving you to see after our Gary. 'e's yorn, you know. Come into t' bedroom. Ee, Gary, it's the nurse what brought yer into t' world, don't yer recognize 'er

— course yer don't, yer poor li'le bugger,' and she squeezed him into her arms. ''E's proper poorly, I'm afraid,' she said, as he wheezed and coughed. The air smelt strongly of camphor. Pearl must have noticed me sniffing, 'Yes, I've give 'is chest a reet good do with Vick; I 'ope I did t' proper thing.' She looked at me anxiously.

'It won't have done him any harm,' I said. Although there were two beds in the room, a double and a single, I noticed that Gary was in the larger one. Again Pearl answered my unasked question, 'I'm sharing my bed with 'im while 'e's bad, it's a treat for 'im, ain't it, Gary?' The boy nodded. 'A bit of luv never comes amiss, and if 'e starts coughing and crying in t' night, I give 'im a cuddle,' she said to me in an almost apologetic aside. I made the pretence of straightening the covers while I examined the bedclothes, which were clean and plentiful. There was no fooling Pearl, 'Oh 'e's warm enough, and there's plenty more blankets if you say 'e should 'ave 'em.'

'No, everything seems to be fine,' I said, and then explained that I was going to give him an injection and that I would be calling twice a day for the same purpose. She seemed pleased, but a little anxious, 'You won't 'urt 'im too much, will yer, nurse?' I promised to be as gentle as I could. She held Gary's hand as I inserted the needle and I'm glad to say he didn't flinch. 'Brave li'le sod, ain't 'e,' murmured Pearl, then before I could agree she said, 'Now let's 'ave a cup of tea and a chat.'

We went into the sitting room and she busied herself

at a gas stove in one corner. In contrast to what I'd seen of the rest of the house, Pearl's two rooms were clean, newly painted and decorated, and comfortably, almost expensively, furnished. Indeed, its appearance was better than most of the homes of patients I visited.

She was a different Pearl from the one I had known six years ago: smartly dressed in polo-necked jumper and slacks, and her hair was obviously well tended, though perhaps a little brassy for my taste. Once again she took my mood, 'Not a bad place, is it? Like me, a bit rough outside but a 'eart of gold inside – to some that is, not all. 'ow about our Gary then, 'e's goin' to be all reet, ain't 'e?' I was able to reassure her on this.

'But . . .' I started.

'I know what yer goin' to say, 'e'd be be'er off in 'ospital. Well, 'e ain't goin'; yer should know what I think of them places by now. You were good enough to bring 'im into this world, so you'll be good enough to keep 'im in it, an' that's that. Now let's talk of summat else.' There was a slight pause, which I broke,

'What are you doing with yourself?'

'Doin' with m'sen? I'm on the game, of course; yer don't think this li'le lot came from working in a shop, do yer?'

I told her I didn't know what to think.

'Well, I 'ope I 'aven't shocked yer. Thought you'd know, anyway. It's as well to be straight, ain't it?'

I supposed it was and I can't deny that I was curious. Pearl was the first prostitute I'd knowingly met, so I thought I might as well use the opportunity to broaden my knowledge.

'What's it like?' I asked innocently.

'Oh, it's a bit up and down, you might say,' she replied with a bawdy laugh. 'Seriously though, nurse, it's no life at all; it's rough and it's dirty. But what was I to do with three kids to bring up – 'and 'em over to the Welfare? Not sodding likely. I may not 'ave wanted the li'le buggers at the time, but now I've got 'em, I luv 'em and I'm goin' to 'ang on to 'em,' she cried defiantly. I glanced round the room. 'I know what yer thinkin', 'ow do I manage with the kids around?' It was getting a little uncanny the way she anticipated my thoughts.

'Well, it had occurred to me,' I admitted, a little grudgingly.

'I've got a friend, Josie, you'll meet 'er sometime. She's busy at the moment; we both use 'er room upstairs, we're partners like. We look after each other and don't need no ponces. Can't stand men, not outside business 'ours anyway. Not that I'm a lez, like a lot of prossies are, just got no feelin's for 'em any more.' She patted her stomach. 'I seem to be goin' on a bit. Life ain't that bad, there's many wuss off than me.' She glanced round the room, 'I didn't 'ave to buy all this, yer know; it was give me by grateful customers. Sometimes yer get be'er value by takin' things in kind, and it makes the men feel be'er. Most of it's probably bin nicked, but I should worry. Would yer believe it, the painting and wallpapering was done by one of the town councillors. Tuk me a time to work that lot off – mean sod.'

Pearl's heart-to-heart was getting a bit much for me, so I thought I'd switch the subject: 'How are your other two children doing? A boy and a girl, wasn't it?'

'Bluddy great, you'll see for yersen when yer come round this evening. The lad's at the grammar school, got 'is eleven-plus, an' our Emmie will do the same, she's the brightest and she's nowt but nine yet.' I must have looked surprised. 'Ay, I knew it'd shock yer, well, it's not all down t' me I'm afraid. It were like this. I was sittin' in t' pub one Friday night, and this lass came up in 'er uniform, selling the *War Cry*. I sent 'er up, as everyone else does, then give 'er a penny or two. This 'appened on a number of Fridays. Then one night she was waiting outside the pub when I left. The fella I was with was out of 'is mind with drink, so there was no trade that night, an' as 'e staggered away she said, "Mrs Caine, can I have a word with you." I was a bit pissed meself, so I said, "A word with me, luv – you can 'ave a 'undred. Cum up and 'ave a cup of tea." Well, she come, and spent an hour or more tryin' to get me to mend me ways. Then one of the kids woke up and 'ad to be fussed over to get 'im back to sleep. "If you won't give over for your own sake, think of the kids," she said. Well, I told 'er, same as I 'ave you, that if I did give over they'd likely starve and 'ave to go to t' Welfare. That set 'er back a bit, and must 'ave got 'er thinkin'. "I believe I can help," she says. "Ay," I says, "I've 'eard that kind of talk before, but when it comes down to doin' owt it's a different tale." "Can I come and see you tomorrow, when I've had a word with my husband?" "Look," I says, "I don't want the bluddy world knowin' about me, just leave me be, I'll be OK." But she went on about 'elpin', so I tells 'er to come back about ten, after I'd got back from seein' t' kids to school.

'The next day there she was, reet on time. "Well," I says, "fancy seeing you again," nasty like. "I've summat to put to you." "Put away," I says. Well, nurse, the long and short of it was, she and 'er 'usband Ron, who was in the Sally Army too, couldn't 'ave any bairns, so she was prepared to tend mine. She said she would tak 'em and bring 'em back from school, sit with 'em of an evenin', play games with 'em, and teach 'em, provided she and Ron could 'ave 'em at their own 'ome every so often. " 'Ow do I know yer won't put 'em against their mam?" I demanded. She promised she'd never do that. "I'll think about it," I said. "Cum round after tea and I'll give you an answer." Well, t' more I thought, t' be'er it seemed. I looked at it this way – I'd be their dad, earning the money and she could mother 'em when I wasn't around. When she came that evenin' I told 'er I'd give it a try. That was two years gone, and it's worked a treat. Of course I pays 'er, I made that plain from the start. She didn't want to tak the money, but I told 'er straight I wasn't 'aving nowt fer nowt. I know she doesn't keep the money 'ersen, she gives it to the Army. I reckon they deserve it with folk like 'er around.'

I must confess, as much as I might deplore the circumstances, it seemed a splendid arrangement and I said so.

'Who is this wonderful woman?'

''Er name's Paula, an' that's all I'm tellin' yer. She don't want it bandied around any more than I do.'

'Do your children know what your work is?'

'Course the two eldest do – didn't I tell yer they were clever? Don't seem to worry 'em.'

'Don't you think they'll feel more strongly as they grow older?'

'Course they will, an' I should bluddy well 'ope so too. They may get to 'ate me, but that's my worry.'

One other thing interested me, 'If you earn good money, why don't you live somewhere else? Surely you and your friend could afford a better place than this.'

Pearl laughed, 'Course we bluddy could, for what we pay 'ere we could rent a soddin' mansion, but the neighbours would be on to us, then the effin' law, an' we'd be out of business in a week. No, this suits us. 'Sides there's no use settin' up shop where there's no buyers, is there? Anyway Josie and I 'ave got another place in Manchester. When things gets a bit slack 'ere, we do a bit up there. Then the kids go and stay with Paula an' Ron. It's funny when yer think, there was Paula tryin' to get me to give up the game, an' what she's really done is 'elp step up trade.' She didn't laugh as she said this; she could see the irony of the situation. Together we took another look at Gary before I left; he was sleeping comfortably.

That evening, and twice a day, until Gary was on the way to complete recovery, I visited 104 Wharf Street. I met Paula many times; we talked together but it was evident that her interest was in the children. I didn't know if she knew that Pearl had told me her story, so I respected her obvious desire for anonymity. The children were a credit to her. They were quiet and polite, with happy but controlled high spirits. I occasionally joined in one of their games and they were as unselfconscious as any children should be. I agreed with Pearl that the situation worked, and worked well. I don't think it necessary for me to comment on Paula and Ron's behaviour, all I can say is that I've given much more generously to the Salvation Army from the time I met her.

I haven't seen Pearl since, nor have I heard of Paula. There was an occasion when Pearl's name came up; it was about four months after my visits. One evening, when I called at the nurses' centre, I was asked to go and see Evelyn Telford.

'Ah, Nurse Jordan, I understand you recently nursed Gary Caine,' she began, piercing me with her steel-blue eyes.

'Yes,' I replied briefly; I didn't want to comment yet, I thought it better to be drawn.

'I've had a call today from the children's officer. I understand that Gary and two other children live with their mother at 104 Wharf Street.'

Again I replied noncommitally.

'According to the children's officer Pearl Caine, the mother, is a known prostitute. Recently she was arrested in Manchester for soliciting, and the police there have asked for a report. He has tried to gain admittance to No. 104 without success, and no one at that address knows anything about her or the children.'

I smiled inwardly, as I recalled my meeting with the 'janitor' on the ground floor. I could imagine the stone-wall reception any official would get from that monster.

'In your opinion, Nurse Jordan,' Evelyn continued, 'were the children uncared for, or in any moral danger because of the nature of their mother's way of life?'

I then decided to relate my story. As it unfolded I watched the assistant superintendent's face soften and her eyes take on an expression of warmth and compassion. When I had ended she paused for a moment or two, and then said, 'Thank you, nurse, for taking me into your confidence, it's something I shall respect. I shall know how to satisfy the children's officer without arousing his curiosity. We don't want the heavy hand of officialdom crushing uncommon humanity, do we?'

Chapter Seven

I suppose it's a fair generalization to say that children grow up in everyone else's eyes except those of their parents, and that grandchildren continue to remain as babies to their grandparents. That was the attitude of Mrs Edith Lawson, and as it was thought at one time that the king could do no wrong, so it was with her children and their offspring. She was not the only patient that I looked after who behaved in the same way and strangely, though usually, it was the attitude of parents who had devoted their lives to seeing that their children were given every opportunity to 'better themselves', those who scraped, saved and did without, so that their sons and daughters could step up into another class. This too was the case with Edith Lawson, with for her, at any rate, not very happy results.

She was the patient of Hugh Morton, one of Burrowdale's younger doctors, of whom it could be said, 'Physician heal thyself', for he suffered from chronic asthma. Although it had interfered with his training (his ambition had been to become a consultant psychiatrist), it did not affect his work as a GP, for as if to compensate for his disability, he drove himself harder than any of his other colleagues. He lived for his work, and his interest in his patients was not confined to their ailments; he could give a biography of any one of them.

The entry in my case-book read: Mrs Edith Lawson, 62 Stream Street. Osteoarthritis. Give general nursing care. Age, seventy-five. What curt references we were given to lives that for those who had lived them had been so very full and important! They were as brief, and flat almost, as the words that would eventually be inscribed on their tombstones.

When I drew up in my car by a shabby terraced house and glanced up at the windows, I was reminded of a saying of my mother's, 'You can always tell decent people by their windows; good-looking curtains and clean panes are an outward sign of the inward and spiritual grace of the people who live in any house'; needless to say, our windows, both outside and in, were a shining example of her creed. If what my mother said was true, I felt I was in for a sad time at No. 62; filthy net curtains, trying vainly to meet in the middle, were strung loosely across the downstairs window and two worn and faded pull curtains looked likely to crumble if any attempt were made to draw them. There was no sound from the rusty doorbell, so I flapped the letterbox and banged on the door, in the hope of making someone hear. After several goes there was an impatient 'OK, OK, I'm coming', and I heard the approach of the music of a rock and roll group. As the door opened, the music blared at me from a transistor radio carried by a mini-skirted, teenage girl made up to look over the age of consent. She was chewing, which gave her face a lopsided expression; she grimaced as her tongue tucked the gum between teeth and cheek.

'Wad daya want?' she demanded.

'Does Mrs Lawson—' I began. She interrupted.

'Oh, our gran, well, she's upstairs, front.'

I made my way there, and as I reached the landing I was wondering how any girl could tolerate the dust, the musty smell and the cobwebs, without attempting to do something about them, and I mentally made a note to book a home help, whose unfortunate job it would be to make the place clean and habitable. Edith Lawson must have guessed my thoughts from my expression, for when I opened the door and looked at the frail, pinched face, she greeted me with, 'Hallo, nurse, I'm reet sorry about the state of the house, but I'll put it to rights the moment I'm on my feet again.' As I examined her gnarled fingers, watched the spasms of pain that she tried so hard to suppress, listened to the familiar creaking of her arthritic joints as she attempted to sit up in bed, and smelt the urinous odour peculiar to arthritic patients, particularly when their hygiene is neglected, I was convinced that this dear old lady would never be on her feet again.

I asked who was looking after her.

'Ellen, the one that opened the door for you. Ever so

good she is, she's one of my grand-daughters. Ee, I'm so lucky with my family.'

I interrupted her, went to find Ellen, and gave her a list of the things I needed. Sulkily she tore herself away from her radio, and appeared two minutes later with a dirty-rimmed white enamel basin of warm water, a spongy, slippery face cloth and a small cracked piece of soap. She picked up a damp hand towel from the chest of drawers, slung it on the bed and with a 'That's it, then' returned to her transistor. I followed her out.

'I need some clean sheets and pillowcases; where are they?' I asked.

'Ah know nowt about them,' she threw at me, as she went downstairs.

After some searching I found what I needed, and returned to my patient.

'A great 'elp is our Ellen, don't you think, nurse?' said the old lady.

I wasn't certain whether it was meant as a statement, or if she wanted reassuring. I made a grunt of acquiescence.

'Ah'm so glad you like 'er, 'cos she's lookin' after me so well – in the daytime that is. Ah don't need anyone at night, of course. In any case she must 'ave some life, mustn't she?'

I wasn't quite sure whether I agreed with her over that.

'What about your children, do they come and see you?' I asked.

'Course they do, whenever they can. Ah've four you

know, two sons and two daughters. And eight grand-children,' she said proudly.

'When was one of them last here?'

'Well, that ah can't recall – not so long back, but they're all that busy, you know. Ee, they 'ave done well, and what with working so 'ard, they can't get away as often as they'd like.'

So it went on, she extolled their virtues and side-stepped any implied criticism. To listen to her was to believe that she and her husband had produced the finest family unit in Burrowdale. They had given up a great deal to see that their children had been well educated, and their sacrifices had been rewarded. To see her in that sordid room, to hear her old joints cracking as she moved, was to know that she lived in a dreamland. She wanted and worked hard to believe it had all been worth while and that she had been repaid, and she succeeded in convincing herself that this was true.

When I had finished my duties and had settled Edith as comfortably as possible, I told her that I would be calling again that evening. 'You'll let yourself in, won't you? I don't suppose Ellen will be 'ere then.' I suggested that it would be as well if she had the services of a home help, and that I would arrange for one to call. 'No, nurse, it's kind of you, but I must refuse. My children would never agree to it. They've told me that as long as I live they'll look after me and see that I want for nothin'.' I decided not to pursue the matter, for the time being, anyway; I would report to Doctor Morton and see what he suggested.

As I left the house a woman came to the door of No. 60.

'Don't think I'm interfering like, nurse, but 'ow is she?'

'Not so good, I'm afraid,' I answered.

'It's that family of 'ers. They keeps 'er a bluddy prisoner, they do. They won't let me near 'er, yet she's a kind owd body really. It's my opinion they want rid of 'er, she's left alone all night, you know. I listens out just in case, but I can't be awake all the time, can I?'

I agreed noncommittally, and thanked her.

I continued my calls, and it was two days before I was able to see Doctor Morton; it was not something I thought could be discussed over the phone. When I'd finished my story, he mused for a while.

'Nurse,' he said, 'there's not a chance of getting her, or her family, to accept the services of a home help. It was lucky that she allowed you in her house. She was a parishioner at Holy Trinity Church, and, when she could no longer attend services, the vicar visited her regularly at home. Eventually he was barred because he sent some of his Young Wives group to help to clean up her house. She has this family fixation, it's partly of her own making and has been encouraged by her children. If we attempt to destroy it by coercing her in any way, we shall take away what she regards as the purpose of her life. She hasn't a lot of time left, let us leave her with a little faith in something.

Your function now is to keep her as comfortable as possible under the circumstances.'

I had to agree with him, and I left feeling somewhat happier. At least now I could see the case in some kind of perspective.

When I called on Edith that evening, I was surprised and delighted that the door was answered by a youngish, well-dressed man, who spoke with what in Burrowdale would be called a posh accent. 'I'm David Lawson, nurse,' he announced. 'Please go on up, my mother is expecting you.' It was a changed Edith Lawson that greeted me; her eyes were sparkling and she bubbled with happiness and excitement. 'That's our David you've just met. Isn't 'e a gradely looking lad, just like 'is dad, and so clever too. I towd you nurse, didn't I, what a grand family I have.' I spent a jolly half hour with her, then said my adieus and went downstairs.

David was in the hall waiting for me, 'I wonder if I could have a word with you, nurse?' He opened the sitting-room door. I went in and sat down. When, like some town councillor, he began thanking me for all I had done and for the care and kindness I had shown to his mother, I began to get suspicious.

'Which brings me to the point of this conversation,' he went on. 'My brother and sisters and I have been discussing the situation upstairs,' he rolled his eyes to the ceiling, 'and we have come to the conclusion that Mother would be much better off in Northerly Hospital.'

I was aghast. Northerly was, to anyone living in Burrowdale at that time, only second worse than the workhouse had been twenty years before. Indeed it was the old workhouse building, and the few modern wings that had been added had done little to alter its austere and bleak appearance. I knew that inside some things had been changed, but that little old lady upstairs didn't. To her it could only mean one thing. It would also mean the destruction of her dreamworld, and that she would die of a broken heart. I began to tell David so. I didn't get very far.

'I'm sorry, nurse, I'm afraid this is our concern, and our concern only. The family are agreed and steps have been taken for her early admittance. We are also agreed that it will not be necessary for you to attend my mother again.'

Dejected, but angry, I left the house and drove round to Doctor Morton. I caught him before his evening surgery. I ended my tale with a sigh of 'God forgive them'. The doctor sat polishing his glasses. He looked up.

'He may not, but their mother will.'

'Why, what do you mean? She's bound to know what they've done to her.'

'I don't think so, nurse. I shall be telephoning Mr David Lawson this evening. I shall tell him that he will inform his mother that it is on my instructions, and on my instructions alone, that she is to be admitted to Northerly. I shall also tell him that unless he makes this plain to her, I shall refuse to sign the necessary admittance papers for his mother; in fact I've no option but to sign them, but he won't know that. Then I shall visit Edith Lawson and give her the news first hand. So don't you worry, the dear lady will be left with her dreams.'

As I drove away, I thanked God for the kind of people that it was my privilege to work with, and for a job that gave me glimpses into the human soul.

It was in a different mood that six weeks later I read in the obituary column of the local paper: 'Edith Mary Lawson, peacefully in hospital, the dearly beloved mother of David, James, Mary and Gladys, and treasured grand-mother of Robert, William, Edward, Jane, Grace, Francis, Jennifer and Ellen. Always in our thoughts.'

Chapter Eight

People's reactions to suffering, pain or blood may vary in strange ways and in degree, yet to nurses there are either good patients or bad, and there's no telling into what category anyone will fall until you have to treat them. I had a friend once who was a patient in my ward, when I was a staff nurse in Ireland. She'd always seemed a sensible, reasonable creature, but from the moment she was admitted she changed. She was constantly complaining, was rude to the nurses, and was unfriendly to the other patients. Her operation was a minor one, causing little pain, yet she groaned her way through her entire stay. I was so ashamed of her conduct that I could hardly bring myself to speak to her afterwards.

Some reactions, though, can be comic. One Saturday evening a number of us nurses, with husbands and boyfriends, had gathered for a jolly at The Mermaid, our out-of-town retreat where we could let our hair down without being accused of disgracing the uniforms we weren't even wearing. 'Busty' Clarke had brought along a new boyfriend, Fred Pickering. Fred was a burly ox of a man, a blacksmith at the local steel works, whom that same afternoon Colin and I had watched playing rugby for Burrowdale, leading the pack and slaughtering the opposition. Inevitably the conversation turned to shop talk, and a theatre sister from the local hospital began describing a particularly rare operation that she'd seen performed during the week. I suppose she was rather graphic, and perhaps a little gory in her detail, but she held everyone's attention. The surgeon was just stitching up the patient when there was an almighty crash as Fred Pickering fell to the floor, taking two or three glasses with him. Everyone's immediate reaction was that he had had a coronary. We loosened his collar and tie, and 'Busty' was about to give him the kiss of life when he opened his eyes, looked around and staggered to his feet. We helped him into a chair.

'There's nowt wrong with me,' he said, 'but don't you start on that sort of thing again,' and he pointed at the theatre sister. 'Bluddy fiendish story, that,' he added sheepishly, but defiantly. 'Now someone can get me another pint, and we'll change the subject,' and he glared round at us. The men kept silent, they weren't risking his possibly violent reactions, but we nurses all burst out laughing.

'Never mind, luv,' 'Busty' said, 'I was going to give you the kiss of life, now I'll give you the kiss of your life instead,' and she locked the scarlet-faced Fred into her embrace.

There was also the case of PC Percy Brown, the pride

of the Burrowdale force, in his own eyes at any rate. He was a big, boyish character, an ex-boyfriend of 'Busty's', whom I'd met once or twice. I remember smiling when I saw his name in my case-book, and thinking that this was one I could have swapped with her a few months earlier. I mentioned it to 'Busty', whose response was direct and to the point, 'Sherlock bloody Holmes! You're welcome to him; solved every crime in Burrowdale, that one has, and a few more besides. He fights gangs single-handed, walks into loaded revolvers. What's wrong with him? Knife wound in the back, I suppose.' I told her that I had to give him penicillin injections for a chest infection. 'If you'll hang on I'll go and get you my specially blunted needle. A few injections with that should stop him talking through his arse for a bit.' Once 'Busty' got steamed up she could go on for ever, so I beat a hasty retreat.

When later that morning I called on Percy, his mother showed me to his bedroom. 'He's very poorly indeed,' she told me. He looked it. He was lying in bed, hunched in the foetal position, his brow hot and sweaty, his hair tousled, and the black bristles of his unshaven face gave him the appearance of a pit collier. He didn't move as Mrs Brown and I entered the room, he just gave a sigh, ending with an imitation death rattle in the throat. 'The nurse is here to see you, Percy,' said his mother gently. He raised his head slightly and opened his eyes, 'Oh, it's you,' he muttered uncomplimentarily, and dropped his head back into the pillow.

'All right Mrs Brown,' I said in dismissal, 'I'll look after him.' When the door closed, I moved towards the bed. 'Well, Percy, and what's the matter with you?'

'Ee, I do feel bad, luv, I ache all over and I've got this hacking cough,' and he proceeded to demonstrate it.

I took my thermometer out of my bag.

'Come on, sit up and put this in your mouth,' I ordered.

He had indeed got a temperature, but it was nothing out of the ordinary for such a case. 'The first thing you've got to do, my lad, is to get yourself cleaned up.' I reached for his dressing gown at the end of the bed, 'Here, put this on, go to the bathroom and have a wash and shave.'

'Do you really think I should?' he said anxiously.

'Of course you should, and you'll feel a lot better for it.'

He returned, looking a deal more presentable. He made for the bed.

'Don't get in there yet,' I ordered. 'Just come over here under the light.' I positioned him. 'That's right, stand there. Take your dressing gown off. Now drop them.'

For a second he stood stock-still and at attention, as if I were a gunman threatening him from behind. Then he turned.

'Drop what?' he demanded.

'Your trousers.'

'Why?' he protested.

'Because I'm going to give you an injection in your behind,' and I showed him the hypodermic syringe I had at the ready.

'You're not going to put that needle in my arse,' he cried. It seemed now that all his other symptoms had disappeared, and had been replaced by fear.

'I certainly am. Twice a day, for the next five days, so drop your trousers, there's a good lad.'

He stood hesitantly, his fingers at the knot of his pyjama cord.

'Hurry up, I haven't got all day and you don't need to worry, I'm sure I've seen many better ones than you've got in my time.' His trousers dropped to his ankles. 'Now bend down.' He obeyed. I took a bit of the flesh of his right buttock between finger and thumb; it was where I would insert the needle. He jumped like a fire cracker.

'Bluddy hell, that hurt.'

'The needle hasn't touched you yet,' I cried.

He bent again, with the same result, this time I followed him. It was like trying to catch a duck. Every time I got near his tail he waddled off, his feet caught up in his pyjama trousers. Finally he flung himself across the bed, I quickly grabbed his flesh, the needle went in and with a groan Percy admitted defeat.

'There,' I said, 'it wasn't too bad was it?'

He shook his head and clambered between the covers. Penicillin injections have a delayed after-effect, a dense pain, seconds later. When this hit him, Percy lurched on his stomach and howled.

'You're a great big baby,' I told him before I left. 'You've wasted a lot of my time and I don't want a repetition of this behaviour when I visit you this evening.' A 'Sorry, nurse luv' was all he could muster, I think he was near to tears. So was I, and so was 'Busty' when I told her!

The incident also came in handy some time later. An elderly patient had asked me if I would post his football coupon, a heavy responsibility! It would have been just my luck, if I'd forgotten, that he would have hit the jackpot. In between calls I drove to the general post office to find there was no parking space. Knowing I would only be a minute or two, I double parked. I'd just bought a postal order and was putting it in the envelope when I heard an authoritative voice say, 'Is the owner of a mini minor in here, please?' I looked up and saw that the voice belonged to Percy. 'It's mine,' I called to him. He looked at me, and showing no signs of recognition said, 'Will you come outside, please.' As I followed him, I took a biro pen from my handbag.

'Well, nurse,' at least now he acknowledged who I was, 'you realize don't you—'

'Turn round and drop 'em, Percy,' I interrupted, pointing the biro at him.

He coloured up, then burst out laughing. 'All right, you win,' he said, 'but move this car quickly, otherwise there'll be trouble.'

I wasn't going to leave without completing my errand, and with him in command.

'I've just got to go back and post this letter, now you

be a good boy and guard my car while I'm away. I'll be back in a jiffy.'

I didn't give him time to reply. When I returned he was half leaning on my mini, 'By the way, nurse, did you read about the case of breaking and entering in Main Street that I—'

'Sorry, Percy,' I said, as I got into my car, 'I haven't time. I've a sick patient to attend to. Tell me later, eh,' and I drove smartly away, leaving him in a cloud of dust and exhaust fumes.

I think that perhaps the bravest patient I have ever nursed was Alec Cox, and I believe that every one of my colleagues in Burrowdale who were called on to care for him, and there were many, would echo my feelings. Without doubt he was the most popular patient for the nine months that we were privileged to treat him. He suffered pain with courage and dignity. He could always raise a smile, even when discomfort turned to agony, and was able to describe what we knew was excruciating pain as, 'It's hurting just a little now. Don't worry it will soon pass.'

In one way Alec was lucky; a bachelor of thirty-nine, he lived with his young married sister and her husband, Betty and Bill Fairfax. Also sharing the semi-detached home was the youngest of his family, brother John. Betty and Bill had two daughters, aged seven and five, and while I was visiting the house, Betty gave birth to a son who was christened Alexander Anthony, but was known to all as 'young Alec'.

I have had published in a medical journal a case study on Alec Cox, under the title 'Carcinoma of maxillary sinus', written in detailed and exact medical terms, which even if I were to transcribe literally would make difficult reading. I hope therefore I may be excused by any members of the medical profession if, in putting this story in plainer terms, I offend their ethical standards.

Alec had cancer, which spread from the top of the right side of his nose to his cheek and upper lip, and later affected the brain, spine and kidneys. I think I should start by describing his case from the beginning, since only by the full knowledge of it can the courage and fortitude of the man be fully appreciated.

The first symptoms were felt some two and a half years before he came into my care. It all began when, feeling an obstruction in his right nostril, Alec thought about visiting his doctor, but it wasn't until his right eye began watering profusely, that he went to him. Doctor Morton sent him to the Ear, Nose and Throat consultant at our local hospital, and x-ray pictures showed that the nostril was blocked by a malignant growth. He was referred to the Holt Radium Institute in Manchester, and spent ten weeks there as an in-patient. There can be no doubt that Alec then knew the nature of his disease. Shortly after he was discharged from the hospital he was able to start work again in the shipyards, though he continued to visit

Manchester every two months for radium treatment, as an out-patient. About six months later his right eye began to pain him, and he found he couldn't see properly with it. Unfortunately the radium treatment had affected the eye, and though all efforts were made to save it, eventually it had to be enucleated, and later he was fitted with an artificial eye. Once more he returned to work. Another six months later he experienced pain in his left cheek, and when he was examined, it was also found that his right cheek was more swollen than when he had last been seen. Within another two months his mouth became ulcerated and a recurrent tumour was diagnosed. It was found that in view of the extensive nature of the disease, further active treatment was no longer feasible, and all that could be done was to keep him as comfortable as possible. He still continued working despite the fact that by now it must have been apparent to him that his condition could only get worse and that, short of a miracle, his days were numbered. The miracle didn't happen. Further swelling of his right cheek made it impossible for him to wear his artificial eye. Not long after this the pain became so severe that Doctor Morton ordered him to bed and he was started on morphine injections.

It was now that I was called in to administer these injections, and to dress his face when necessary. It was now, too, that I began to get the measure of this remarkable man. His manner towards me at the beginning of our association was reticent, though he was grateful for the relief the injections gave, and apologetic for the trouble he thought he was causing. I found this reticence understandable. I was another milestone nearer the end of his journey. He also refused to allow me to attend to his dressings. I accepted this as pride on his part; he didn't want the ugliness of his face exposed to me. 'My sister sees to them for me, nurse, if you don't mind.' I did mind, but I wasn't going to say so yet; I decided to get to know his sister first.

Betty was twenty-eight, a bright, busy, charming young woman, with what mother-in-laws describe as 'sensible looks'. I found she was anxious to tell me all about her brother and his story, as she saw it. What emerged, without her relating it, was the family's devotion to Alec, a devotion in deeds as much as in words. From the moment that he was confined to bed, it was decided that come, what may, he would remain at home with them until his death. The burden of responsibility was to be shared, though it was recognized that most must fall on Betty. They were fortunate in that the house had four bedrooms. Alec was moved to the large back bedroom, from where he could gaze down on to the garden that he had once looked after. His room was also next door to the lavatory and bathroom. In order that Betty could always have a man in the house in case of emergencies, the younger brother transferred to the nightshift. Everything was geared to Alec's comfort, and the happiness of his remaining days. Even the two young children caught the spirit of the thing, they played and tumbled around him, joked with him, and when the wounds in his face became hideous they seemed never to notice or to flinch from them.

When Betty's baby was due and Doctor Morton suggested that it might be easier if Alec went into hospital for a time, so that she could have a home confinement, she wouldn't hear of it, and it was she that went to the hospital. I'm glad to say that by then Alec had so many people around him who were willing to help that her absence was compensated for.

I found it easy to be able to persuade Betty that it would be wiser if I did Alec's dressings. It was subtly arranged, with her first calling for my assistance and later saying that she didn't feel able to cope properly.

A television set was of course installed in his room and it was something that was to affect the lives of all those around him, for Alec got to love the horses, and became an inveterate gambler, though with the smallest of stakes; a bob each way was his limit. He read *Sporting Life* from cover to cover each day, and would drag me in on deciding which horses to back, 'You're Irish, nurse, and the Irish know all about the horses. Now I've narrowed it down to three possibles, which of them do you think will win?' He didn't always follow my advice, which was just as well. It seemed that God, who had frowned on him, was determined to make some amends, and Alec had many a run of good luck. Not that he worried when he lost; it was the thrill, the excitement, the laughs that went with it, that he enjoyed, and so did we all. At that time there were no betting shops, and the local bookies' runner, Joe O'Connor, would call round for the bets, and to deliver the winnings.

Joe was of course an Irishman, and he grew to love Alec and would make any excuse to come and be with him. He shared the bits of information he had: 'There's a lot of money going on this one today'; or, 'The Governor doesn't want any money on him, must be a reason.' Gradually everyone around got drawn into the racing game, friends, workmates, Doctor and Mrs Morton (Mrs Morton was a frequent visitor), the vicar (though with him we were sworn to secrecy), and even the local constable. This of course delighted Joe:

'Now you're in on it, Bill, you'll niver be able to lay a finger on me.'

'Don't you be too sure,' Bill replied.

'Sure? Sure I'm sure. See, here's one of your slips,' and he pulled a bit of paper out of his top pocket, 'I didn't hand this one in. I'm glad to say it didn't win, and it's got your monicker on it. What would the beaks say to that, eh?'

Then followed a game of hunt the slipper (or the slip), with Bill trying to destroy the evidence. It ended up under Alec's pillow, which of course was out of bounds to everyone.

Often when he had a win it would be boxes of chocolates for the nurses, and cigarettes for the men; when I rebuked him for his extravagance and told him that he should be saving up his money for a rainy day, he'd say,

'That's just what I've done, you see it's raining outside, yet the smile on your face is as warming to me as if the sun was shining.'

During the summer there would be flowers all round the room, and his friends from the shipyards cultivated his allotment, 'just to keep it going for you Alec', and they would bring vegetables and fruit, most of which was later given to visitors. Alec of course by now was unable to eat. Drinking, too, was difficult, though he managed this with the help of drinking straws. The fluids were varied: Complan, Horlicks, Ovaltine, soups and the like. As an everyday diet they were expensive. Alec knew this, and since he was proudly independent, for a time he gave up gambling on the horses, but even this small saving wasn't sufficient for his needs. I suggested to Betty that she should apply for National Assistance for him. She came back from the office white and shaken; she'd been told, and told harshly, that she had no right to apply for their help, as there was enough money going into the house already to provide for him. I took up the cudgels and went to see the inspector. I got the same treatment. I decided to hand over to Mrs Mac. I listened, as she first cajoled and then losing her temper gave forth the strongest bit of Scottish invective it was ever my pleasure to hear. She then applied to the Society for Cancer Relief, who gave generously and without question. While we were of course grateful and delighted for their help, as Mrs Mac put it, 'In a way it makes the behaviour of the Assistance people harder to bear. We know only too well how they naïvely hand over money to scroungers, rogues and liars, yet when we support a genuine case, they start playing it by the book. Niver ye mind though, ah'll get my own back on that inspector, nay matter how long I have to wait.' She did, too, but that's another story. It was of course never explained to Alec where the money really came from, he assumed it was just an addition to his sick pay.

Alec's condition, as we all knew, could only deteriorate. The cancer which had started at the top of his nose had gradually eaten away his right nostril, and continued down the right side of his face and upper lip, until there was no tissue left. What had been his cheek was a gaping hole, which daily had to be swabbed with sterile water and packed with gamgee: cotton wool between two layers of gauze. The left side had also been attacked, a scarlet mass had formed over the lower jaw bone and there was the continual fear that this too would break down. As his face was eaten away, Alec had several severe haemorrhages, which would have been terrifying to a lesser man, as indeed they were to his sister. My colleagues and I were always ready to answer an urgent call, so was Doctor Morton, but Betty often had to cope until we arrived. She nevertheless remained adamant that Alec would stay in the house until he died, and despite his deteriorating condition, we encouraged her in this; to move him now would be like taking him to his grave. 'How is it going to end?' Betty would entreat us, but no one could tell.

By now his regular three injections a day were often insufficient, and Betty had to be trained to give additional ones, should they be required during the night. Doctor Morton had also prescribed a special mixture, 'Alexander Cocktail' as he jokingly called it; in fact it contained both gin and morphine. It produced a feeling of euphoria, and when it was first given it was prescribed in small measures, for use in between injections. Eventually, Doctor Morton told Alec to help himself whenever he felt like it, and not to worry about amounts. 'Swig as much as you feel you want,' were his instructions.

During the last fortnight of his life, Alec's condition worsened rapidly. The disease was now affecting his spine and kidneys and there was the imminent danger that the eating-away process on his face would corrode the jugular vein at the side of his neck, and so cause a massive haemorrhage. Yet his cheerfulness still prevailed, though his torn mouth could only register a twisted smile.

One afternoon, when I visited him, the whole situation had changed. Betty told me the story. At about two o'clock Alec had asked her to help him to the lavatory. Together they struggled towards the door, but it was too much, he couldn't make it and defecated in his pyjamas. His spirit snapped. For the first time since his illness he broke down and cried. His sobbing wracked his emaciated body and Betty had to take him in her arms like a child, to get him back into bed. Telling the tale took the same toll on Betty, whose tears were uncontrollable.

I telephoned for Doctor Morton, and made my way alone to Alec's room. This then was the end. I knew that if nature didn't see that it was, the doctor would. When the will to fight has left such a man, death should, and indeed must, follow fast. It is like the last cry from the cross, '*Eli, eli lama sabachthani*; My God, my God, why hast thou forsaken me?'

When Doctor Morton arrived he immediately gave Alec an injection of pethidine, for with his resistance at an end, pain took over. It was a dose from which he knew Alec could not recover. Perhaps it could be interpreted as euthanasia. But what is a doctor to do? How can he tolerate seeing a man lying there, screaming in pain, when he knows he has a drug that can prevent it, even though he is aware it will terminate his life? I stayed with Alec and so did his family, who had by now assembled, and we watched as unconscious he moved towards death; his breathing became slower and shallower, and at seven-forty he died peacefully and without drama.

I may be accused of writing about this case to satisfy people's morbid fascination. This has not been my intention. I have done it to illustrate a man's courage and endurance, and the support the loving kindness of a family can give. I also hope that it shows the feeling of achievement and fulfilment there is in nursing cases, even where death is inevitable.

There is one other observation that I would like to make on a situation that came about as a result of this case. Alec had brought a number of people together, who had seen the ravages that cancer can cause, at first hand; his death left a gap which we decided could be partly filled by our working together, to raise money for the Cancer Relief Fund. We co-operated happily in this way for a year, and were able to send a number of small cheques to the charity. Other organizations in Burrowdale offered their support, which was impossible to refuse, then gradually they took over, until the original spirit which had prompted our efforts was lost. It was no longer 'Our Alec's' fund, it had lost an identity founded on our love and pride for a gallant man. It seemed a pity.

Chapter Nine

Daphne Wise was perhaps the brightest, prettiest and liveliest of our district nurses. She joined about a year after me, and as I did, took on relief midwifery duties from time to time. We quickly became friends. I think she enjoyed being able to confide in an older woman and I suppose I was flattered that she had selected me. When I first saw her I remember thinking, 'You won't be with us long,' not because I thought she wouldn't be able to stand the work, but I was sure some man would whisk her quickly to the altar. She did have many men friends and for Burrowdale lived what I would call a full social life, which I enjoyed second-hand. Occasionally it was embarrassing, for sometimes I would meet her boyfriends, who would say, 'I don't think we've met before, nurse,' and to whom I felt like replying, 'No, but I reckon I know more about you than your own mother.' Sometimes it could be a bit off-putting, because people's reactions to the same person can be entirely different, and preconceived ideas can get in the way.

I was wrong in thinking that she soon would be married.

One year followed another, and Daphne still remained single, and quite untroubled about it. 'Why should I go rushing into marriage?' she said to me one day, when I taxed her about her bird-like attitude towards men, flitting as she did from tree to tree. 'If ever a job showed you the folly of that sort of behaviour, this one does. No, I believe in shopping around. I've sorted through a few of the fellows in Burrowdale,' she said with a twinkle.

'Yes, but so far you've found no one to fit,' I replied. 'It seems to me the more you sort through, the choosier you become.'

'You wait and see, I'll find the one I want in the end.'

'Yes, and perhaps he won't want you,' I called after her, as she left for yet another new date.

She was incorrigible. One or two of the older nurses foretold a gloomy future for her, 'She's riding for a fall, that young lady,' they said as they tut-tutted together. It was some months after this particular exchange between us that I noticed a change in Daphne. When we met she seemed less communicative, more absorbed in herself. We chatted together, but there were none of the confidences I'd been accustomed to. I wasn't worried for her, since she seemed happy enough, in a reflective sort of way.

One evening after duty I went into the nurses' sitting room and there was Daphne in her coat ready to leave. She looked up at me and her face lit, she was radiant. She jumped to her feet, ran over and put her arms round me.

'Pat,' she said, 'I've been waiting for you. I wanted you to be the first around here to know. Look!' and she snatched off her left-hand glove; there on her third finger was a diamond and sapphire ring.

'You're engaged!' I said, a trifle unnecessarily.

'Yes,' she grabbed me by the arm, 'come and sit down and I'll tell you all about it.' With that she pushed me into the sofa, and began.

Well, I don't want to be unkind to her, but it was the sort of stuff that I had heard many times before from girls in the first flush of triumph at capturing their man. Briefly it went as follows: Daphne, some three months before, had met a naval lieutenant, whose ship was in the yards for a refit – 'He was so different,' she said, 'not one of the run-of-the-mill Burrowdale men. I knew at once he was the one I had been waiting and hoping for. I was ecstatic.' After this she went on a bit. Their relationship grew close, but then stood still – Senior Service – silent service, he loves me – he loves me not, when will he put the question? Spirits up – spirits down. I was beginning to get impatient.

'How did you get him in the end?'

'Sheer bloody professionalism,' she replied. 'One evening he complained that he'd a bad cold. He had got the sniffles a bit, but from the way he went on you'd have thought he had pneumonia. Well, I played up to him, I put him into my bed, rang his ship telling them he was worse than he was, at the same time pulling the nurse bit. They seemed impressed. I told them I was getting in touch with a doctor and that I thought he should stay where he was for the present. They agreed, "We don't want everyone here down with flu." Then I got Doctor O'Dea round and let him into my secret; he fussed around and when he left his parting words to Jim were, "You're in very good hands, lieutenant, Nurse Wise will soon pull you through."

'Well, of course from that moment I gave him the full treatment, Florence Nightingale would have been proud of me. I began bullying him a bit, and he loved it. I could see that he was looking at me through new eyes. When he thought he was strong enough, he tried to drag me into bed with him. I did the big resistance act, "We're not well enough for that sort of thing," I told him primly. "Now just you be a good boy, we don't want your temperature rising again, do we?" His eyes almost welled over with tears, it was then I knew I'd got him, hook, line and sinker. Two hours later he popped the question. By now I'd got the bit between my teeth, "You must be feverish," I said. The more I protested the more he contested, and this is the result.' She raised her left hand and flashed the ring at me again. 'All right, I may be marrying a bloody hypochondriac, but he's the one for me.'

The mention of marriage brought me back to earth. 'Have you fixed the day?'

'That's just it,' she said, bright-eyed and shining, 'he's joining another ship in a month's time. He can get a fortnight's leave for the honeymoon, so that means the wedding will have to be on Saturday week.'

'You'll be coming back to work after of course.'

'Not likely, I shan't. Jim's got a small house near South-ampton that his father left him. I shall be spending my time getting that "ship-shape" as Jim says, while he's away on his next trip. I'll be married here though, so that you girls can enjoy the fun.'

'But what about the month's notice you're expected to give? Have you told Mrs Mac yet?' That brought Daphne up with a jolt.

'Oh, my Gawd, I'd forgotten about her; you don't think she'll mind though, do you?'

I didn't have to think about it, and Daphne must have seen the way my face had gone, because she began mut-tering uncomplimentary things about the Scots.

'She needn't think I'm afraid of her,' she said, showing she was scared stiff. 'I'll tell her tomorrow morning. Come on, let's go and have a drink to celebrate.'

Over our gins it was agreed that I would be around to give her some kind of moral support. She must have been with Mrs Mac for over a quarter of an hour, which to my reckoning was more than flesh and blood could stand. When she came back into the sitting room she looked as though she'd been put through a mangle.

'Let's hope Jim's worth it,' she said as she sank into a chair.

'Was it that bad?' I murmured sympathetically.

'Worse,' she nodded. 'According to her I've let all my colleagues down, I'm a disgrace to my uniform and the service, and I'm a sex maniac because I can't wait a few months for a man's affection.' Daphne then went off into a string of expletives.

'Never mind,' I comforted, 'it's over now, anyway Mrs Mac's bark is always worse than her bite.'

We heard footsteps coming down the corridor and composed ourselves a little, the door opened and in walked Mrs Mac.

'Ah, Nurse,' she beamed, 'Ah suppose Daphne has been telling ye her good news. Ah'm sure yer as happy for her as I am. It'll mean a few extra duties for all of us for a time, ah'm afraid, but we shan't mind that, shall we?' Then she turned and swept out, humming as she went.

'I thought you said you had a hard time with her,' I murmured sweetly.

'The two-faced bitch,' was Daphne's brief comment.

Daphne's duties had to be divided out, and I got my share of them. We spent a laborious afternoon going through the case history sheets, while she explained the various social, medical and obstetric difficulties that might arise. When we came to one headed 'Mrs Maria Hutton', whose first child was to be born ten weeks later, Daphne gave a wolf whistle.

'What's the matter with her?' I inquired.

'Nothing's the matter with that young lady, in fact she has everything and everybody going for her, I would say.'

'What do you mean?'

Daphne laughed. 'You'll have to find out for yourself, all I can say is that you'll enjoy her.'

We left it at that.

Daphne and her lieutenant were duly married. The reception at The Royal Hotel was a very posh 'do', as they say in the north. It wasn't a 'knife and fork' affair, it was champagne and canapés, with a bevy of naval officers to delight our nurses' contingent. To say Mrs Mac rose to the occasion would be an understatement, she towered over it. The officers, both young and old, seemed captivated by her. 'What a wonderful character; it must be great working under a skipper like that, eh?' were the kind of remarks being heard. We could only agree; to have tried to explain what she was really like would have taken too long, and anyway it would have spoiled the fun. As she kissed the bridegroom good-bye, she was heard to murmur, 'You've taken the pick of my flock, but I forgive you,' which may have made good listening for Jim, but not for some of us older sheep, who were grazing nearby at the time.

It was about four weeks later that as I looked through my week's duties I saw that on the following Thursday I was to give Mrs Maria Hutton an ante-natal examination. Remembering Daphne's remark, I wondered what lay in store for me; then recalling that she'd said I would enjoy the experience I relaxed and looked forward to satisfying my curiosity.

When I arrived at the semi-detached house where

Maria lived, I was favourably impressed with its appearance; newly painted white, with a well-kept garden, sparkling bay windows and heavy lace curtains; it looked what it was, a middle-class, well-kept home. I rang the chiming doorbell and waited. The door was opened by a junoesque woman of incredible loveliness. It was not just her perfect features and skin; she seemed to exude beauty. She was wearing a red tailored housecoat, over which her long black hair cascaded. As I glanced at her figure I thought, 'This can't be my patient.'

'I've called to see a Mrs Hutton,' I said, 'I believe she is expecting me.'

'I am Maria 'Utton, pleez you come inside. You are 'ere to see me instead of Nurse Wise, eh?'

'Yes,' I stammered, 'but. . .'

'I know what it eez you tink. You say to yourself, she is not pregnant, but I am, it eez just zat I carry my bambino well, eh?'

As she turned and walked through the hall I glimpsed the tell-tale bulge, though she moved with the grace and pride of a prima ballerina. She showed me into the living room, where on a snow-white cloth on the table were a bowl, a jug of water and a piece of soap; the things necessary for me when I had concluded my examination.

'I prefer you to examine me down 'ere, it eez so cold in my bedroom at theez time of ze year. Zat couch vill be all right for ze purpose, vill it not?' I agreed. 'But ven you 'ave finished you would like a cup of coffee, eh?' and without waiting for my answer she walked out of the room into the kitchen where I heard her say, 'Pleez my darling Kennet, you maka ze coffee now.' Then a deep English voice replied, 'Of course, my sweetheart. Is there anything else you want?'

'Only one ting.' There followed the sound of a succession of kisses.

Maria returned completely composed and sat down opposite me, while I asked her the usual questions. I'm afraid I didn't pay the attention I should have to her answers, I found it difficult to concentrate, I couldn't take my eyes from her face. I felt that the Mona Lisa had not only come to life, but was sitting there in front of me – pregnant.

I suppose I should explain my absorption. I don't know whether other nurses feel the same way as me, but so often do I have to look at bodies deformed by age, accident or neglect, that when I see perfection of the human form, whether it be in man, woman or child, I get the kind of aesthetic pleasure that others have from music and the arts.

When the moment came for her examination, to my astonishment Maria unzipped her housecoat from top to bottom, moved to the couch, slipped effortlessly on to it, threw her coat apart and exposed her entire body. I was astonished, because generally women are modest in such circumstances, and only raise their maternity frocks to their waists. Maria gave no sense of flaunting herself, it was as if she thought it to be the most natural thing to do, so she lay there, with her breasts and tummy pointing towards the ceiling. When the examination was over, without bothering to refasten her housecoat, she moved back to the chair.

'Eez everyting all right?' she inquired anxiously.

'Yes Mrs Hutton, everything is fine,' I replied.

Her face lit up with pleasure, 'Oh, I must go and tell Kennet, 'e vill be so pleezed, zen I vill bring in ze coffee,' and she left the room, breasts adjutting, with her housecoat flared out like a royal train. I heard her speak to 'Kennet', telling him what I'd said. 'That's wonderful news, my madonna,' then again came the sound of an embrace, followed by, 'No, in your condition you must not carry the tray, I will bring it in.'

Kenneth was almost as handsome as Maria was beautiful: a fair, tall, broad-shouldered Englishman; Nordic where she was Roman, and he had charm. He took over easily as he served the coffee.

'Maria tells me everything is all right, nurse.' It was almost a question.

'Yes,' I replied, 'there seem to be no complications.'

We made conversation for a few minutes, with Kenneth doing most of the talking; Maria seemed almost meek in his presence. As I was about to announce my departure, Kenneth said that he had to go out for a while. At this she became alarmed, 'Oh, my darling, must you go? How long vill you be?' When he said about an hour she put her arms round his neck, 'I shall meez you, *caro mio*, every minute you're away vill seem like an hour; take care, my darling.' Kenneth promised he would take great care.

I must say I found it heady stuff, as well as a little embarrassing. All the same I thought it wonderful that fairytale marriages still existed. When Kenneth left the house I remarked to Maria on her husband's charm.

'But Kennet, 'e eez not my 'usband, 'e eez my lovair,' she explained with a throaty chuckle, 'but as you say, 'e 'as great charm, and eez a beautiful man.'

I wasn't sure what sort of noise to make after this admission. I didn't have to worry; for Maria the flood gates were now open, and she began to tell me her life story, or, rather, her love-life story. Briefly, at the end of the war she had gone from Italy to Germany, where she had worked as a clerk with the allies. It appeared she had fraternized around and so was able to speak French, German and English fluently. Then she met Roy Hutton, a sergeant in the British army, and they got married. She went on to say that while living abroad he had loved her passionately; she hugged her body while telling me this. After their arrival in this country his fiery ardour had gradually cooled off, or as Maria put it, 'Ven I say to 'im, "Roy, you pleeza love me, eh,"'e say, "No, I am too tired." Can you imagine, nurse, any man being too tired to love me?' She said it so simply, it couldn't be taken as conceit. 'So I must, 'ow you say, compensate, I find Kennet and I am a most fortunate woman. I 'ave a good 'usband, and a vonderful lovair.' The way she said it at the time made it sound a most sensible arrangement; she was as persuasive as a happy child.

I visited her every Thursday afternoon for the next few weeks. Kenneth was always there to make the coffee, and usually joined us in our *tête-à-tête*. I was glad when he did, for then Maria didn't talk so much, or so intimately, and it was easier for me to get away.

I learned during those visits that Maria attracted men as a magnet does steel. Although Kenneth was there to answer the door, tradesmen all seemed to want to talk to her, and would keep her on the doorstep on one pretext or another. Once a council official came to discuss a mistake the Huttons had made over the payment of their rates. She showed him into the living room and he began by being almost rude to her. She responded by behaving like a damsel in distress, flickering her long black eyelashes, and speaking in her most broken English, with her ''Ow eez eet you say' and 'Oh you English, you are so clevair, and I am so stupid', so that soon the poor man was apologizing for having worried her; it was all the fault of his department, 'Just leave it to me, I'll sort it out for you.' And as if embarrassed by the stirring of his emotions, gathered together his papers, took one last look into Maria's eyes and fled through the door. I was proud of my sex on that particular occasion.

One Sunday, just as I was about to serve lunch at home, the phone rang and a cultured voice said, 'This is Roy

Hutton, Maria's husband, speaking. I'm sorry to have to trouble you, nurse, on a Sunday, but it looks as though our baby has chosen today to be born.' I chatted with him for a bit about Maria's condition. It wasn't that I was worried about her, I wanted to get some idea what her husband was like before I met him. I felt in a way an accessory after the fact in Maria's illicit relationship.

When I arrived at the house a charming middle-aged lady with a north-country accent opened the door, and introduced herself as Mrs Hutton senior. She took my coat and nursing bag, and accompanied me to the bedroom. Maria was lying in a double divan, with its white padded headboard; everything in the bedroom was white; walls, curtains and carpet. Maria, in perfect contrast, was wearing a scarlet nightdress and her splendid black hair hung in two waist-length braids, fastened with scarlet bows, over the coverlet. She looked lovelier than ever. Her husband, a stocky, dark-haired, swarthy-complexioned man, was sitting close to her, and their hands were clasped as if they were plighting eternal troth. When he saw me he freed himself, shook my hand and welcomed me saying, 'Maria has told me so much about you, nurse, the help you have given and what good company you have been for her.' Then with justifiable pride he showed me into an adjoining room, which had been fitted out as a nursery in the most excellent taste, and with no expense spared. Everything was as perfect as it could be for a home confinement.

Introductions and pleasantries over, I shooed everyone

out of the bedroom, while I examined Maria. I found myself wondering as I did so how her conscience was treating her at this moment. I needn't have worried. 'My Roy, 'e eez so vonderful, so loving, so anxious for me. Am I not lucky, nurse, to 'ave so marvellous a 'usband?' I was able to agree to that, with absolute honesty. ''As 'e told you, nurse, that 'e vants to be present at ze birth of ze baby?' That set me back on my heels. I said a silent prayer that this infant would not be born with fair hair and fair skin; all right, if it was they could sort it out together later, but I didn't want any scenes immediately after the delivery; I couldn't really be sure how much Mr Hutton knew about his wife, and her behaviour. Neighbours anywhere have a habit of talking. It was quite apparent that Roy's parents knew nothing, for they invited me to join them at tea time in the living room, and spoke in glowing terms about their lovely daughter-in-law, and said what a wonderful wife she had been to their son. Indeed, much to my surprise, they went on to say they hoped their grandchild would be a girl, and that she would inherit her mother's beauty. Greater love have no in-laws than this, I thought.

Maria's labour progressed satisfactorily, medically speaking that is. I expect she would have reported it differently, for she became a little hysterical at times. When this happened she clutched her husband tightly, and swore her undying love for him.

The moment came for me to put a routine call through to her doctor; it's usual practice to inform him that his patient 'has started', and to tell him how she is progressing. Jerry O'Dea was Maria's doctor, and with our Irish connection we were on excellent terms both professionally and socially. He showed great faith in my judgement, so that when I was able to tell him that everything looked like being plain sailing for Mrs Hutton, I expected him to give me the usual 'Thank you for telling me, I know she'll be all right in your hands', and forget about the case until Monday morning. It didn't go like that. At the mention of her name, he was all concern. 'Poor little Mrs Hutton,' he murmured into the phone, 'it's her first, isn't it? Yes, well, I think I'll come along, just to make sure everything is all right.' Minutes later I heard his car door slam, he ran up the stairs, then stood gazing down tenderly at her beautiful face, passed his hands over her brow, and finally held her wrist for a lot longer than was necessary to take her pulse. She of course responded as she knew how. He was just another of Maria's victims. He eventually took his leave, having made no proper examination. 'You're in very capable hands, Mrs Hutton,' he said as he went.

At nine-thirty that night Maria's son was born. God had answered my prayer, for he was seven pounds of typical Italian stock. Maria recovered fast, and the torrid love scene that followed would have done credit to a Hollywood spectacular. Roy caressed and kissed his wife, and she responded with every gesture of love and endearment. I was glad when the parents-in-law came in; Roy's mother's, 'Ee, was it very bad, luv?' would I hoped bring everything back to reality. Maria wasn't finished yet though. With a theatrical movement she threw out an arm, clasped Roy's hand, and drawing him to her said, 'No, eet vas quite vonderful because you see I 'ad my Roy viz me all ze time.'

During the fourteen days that followed that passion-laden evening I visited Maria and her baby every day. She was most interested in post-natal exercises, as she was anxious that her figure should not suffer any ill-effects from the pregnancy. It was obvious too that she was going to be a good mother to her child, providing of course that she did not smother him with love.

During this time there was no sign of Kenneth, nor was any reference made to him. Once I did venture what was a loaded remark, by asking her what she intended doing with herself now. She knew what lay behind it because she answered quite haughtily, 'Stay at 'ome of course and be a good mother to my son.' I thought, a trifle bitchily, 'And be a good wife to your husband, I hope.' When the time came for us to say good-bye, she thanked me most affectionately and effusively, and thrust an expensive present in my hand. She asked me to call any time I was passing. It was an invitation I never accepted. I'd seen enough, and enjoyed what I'd seen; there might, I thought, be the danger that what had been a delightful and amusing episode could if taken further have become tarnished and tawdry.

I did however meet Maria once again, about a year later, when I was walking in a street near to her house. I noticed a provocative behind wheeling a high white pram expertly along the pavement. It belonged of course to Maria. Even if I hadn't recognized her, my attention would have been alerted by the whistles of the labourers on the opposite side of the road, They had stopped working, pushed back their caps and were standing in wonderment and appreciation at the mini-skirted delights she bestowed as she wiggle-waggled her way along. Maria responded generously by turning towards them, pouting her lips and flickering her eyelashes.

I caught up with her and she stopped while I admired her baby. She told me the usual things that mothers do about their children, then she bent over the pram and said, 'Say 'allo to ze nurse, Kennet.' She gazed into my eyes with that strange innocent look, then slowly her left lid closed in a wink, and with a 'Good-bye, nurse' she moved out of my life.

Perhaps not completely, though, for I sometimes think of her, when people condemn someone for their infidelity. Adultery, I've come to the conclusion as a result of knowing Maria, is like other sins – it's a matter of degree. It depends so much on who commits it, and how it is committed.

Chapter Ten

'It's a hard and unrewarding task ah'm going to have to put to ye, Patricia,' said Mrs Mac, one summer morning, when I'd answered her summons to the office. 'It must be indeed,' I thought, 'otherwise you'd never be calling me by my Christian name.' I braced myself for the quick-fire orders and instructions that generally followed. They didn't come. She sat with her eyes down, fidgeted with some papers, and was seemingly at a loss for words. This was a Mrs Mac I didn't recognize.

Suddenly she picked up a pencil, stubbed it on her desk and, raising her head, glared at me.

'It's a case of multiple sclerosis,' she barked, as though it was my fault. 'Ah'll tell ye what this case means. It's going to be like a prison sentence for ye, only worse, for ye won't know how long ye'll have to serve, but ye will know that it'll get harder the longer it lasts. All right it's only an hour each day, but it's likely to affect yer attitude to yer other work unless ye're a tougher body than I think ye are. Remember too ye're nay just taking on one patient, in this case a whole family is affected, so though ye'll not be able to cure your patient, ye can make living almost bearable for them. Here are the particulars. Ye start today. Good luck.'

Then she turned her back on me, so indicating that our meeting was over.

As was usual after such visits, I came out stunned, more by the way Mrs Mac had fired her orders, than by the orders themselves. It wasn't until I had time to reflect on what she had said that I realized something of the size of what I was to face in the future. For me, as for most nurses, the driving force of the job was to heal the sick; when dealing with old folk in the throes of senile decay, I felt I was able to make them comfortable in body, and perhaps in spirit and to help them to see their lives out with dignity. As I have shown, even with terminal cancer in its advanced stages there was the knowledge that the patient's suffering would be short-lived, but I realized that with multiple sclerosis, apart from there being no cure, there was no knowing how long a person might continue to suffer, always aware that he is an ever-increasing burden to himself and to those around him, and that anything I would be able to do, or so it seemed to me at that moment, would bring no relief to anyone. I should only be able to stand by and watch the disease get steadily worse and possibly see the break up of a family into the bargain.

The thought of a family brought me back to reality. Who was my patient? I looked at the paper in my hand – Robert Saunders. The name rang a bell. Number 10

Lambton Row, Seaspray. My mind went back over the years. I'd been to Seaspray, and to the Saunders. It was to bandage and attend a six-year-old girl, who'd torn her arm falling off a pony. I checked back through my diaries and confirmed what my memory had made me fear. It was Bob Saunders, the father of that child, who was to be my patient. I remembered the day when I had removed the bandage and pronounced her arm well again, he had been there; a big man with a boyish face, twinkling eyes and an almost devilish sense of fun. I remembered how he'd seized his little daughter, slung her on his back and dashed out into the garden, booming, 'After a fall, after a fall, have no fear, no fear at all. Get right up on that horse's back, take the reins and give them a crack.' Then all of us had dissolved into laughter.

What a happy family they had seemed. His wife, Doreen, was what I would call a handsome, sensible woman, a farmer's daughter from up in the hills, and I remembered how their small house always smelt of baking bread, scones, pies and cakes, the sort of smell that makes you feel hungry, even if you have just had a meal. There had been another elder daughter, whom I hadn't met because she was at school; it seemed a tragedy that fate had treated them so cruelly.

I remembered it all so clearly as I drove up the narrow, windy road to Seaspray, which like so many coastal villages in Cumbria lies where a valley in the hills flares out onto the sea. It was protected by the hills on three sides, but in winter when the wind was blowing over the water it became a wild-looking place seen through a mist of spray and rain that met over it. Today, although it was a sunny summer morning, it gave me little joy.

The house was much the same as it had been those years before. It was one of a row of greystone cottages that stood out from the others with its newly painted look, its gay chintz curtains, and pretty front garden full of bright flowers. As I got out of the car I thought it would be best for everyone if I put on my 'professional manner'. I didn't have time to assume it. The door opened and there was a smiling Doreen coming down the path to greet me. 'Hallo, nurse, how grand it is to see you again; we were told you were coming and Bob is most excited. He remembers the fun we had together, though it must be all of six or seven years ago.' She took me into the sitting room; again it was much as I remembered it, except now there was a single bed in the bay window, put there, as Doreen later told me, 'because Bob likes to watch the flowers grow, and so that he can tap on the window when any of his friends are passing. They always stop to have a chat with him. He saw you the moment your car drew up and shouted at me to let you in.'

Although Doreen hadn't altered, Bob of course had, but only physically. He'd lost several stone in weight, his face was sunken, but his eyes still flashed and there was plenty of the old sense of fun in him. 'It's wonderful to see you, nurse; as I told Doreen, you'll soon have me on my feet again and jumping around like the clumsy horse I was when you last saw me.' Doreen took up his mood, 'Yes, Bob, you're right, we'll soon get you up and about again, though I'm not sure I don't prefer you where you are, I can keep an eye on you now and see you don't get into too much mischief.' And the three of us laughed, as though nothing had changed over the years.

I was however watching them both carefully as they played what they and I knew was a game between them. This then was the way they were living it. It seemed to have worked, judging by Doreen's appearance, and I realized that this was the only way it could be made to work – for the time being at any rate – all that could be done was to live for the day.

I now got on with the job I had been sent to do: to wash and dress the patient, and with the help of Doreen put him in his wheelchair in which he spent the best part of the time. As I did it I studied his condition. Although there are more complete and complicated medical definitions, I should describe disseminated sclerosis as a disease that affects the nervous system; scattered patches of degeneration attack the nerve cells, and destroy them. This causes paralysis; the limbs contract, and any attempt to force them can result in breakage. Another symptom or development is diplopia, double vision, so is incontinence – that destroyer of human dignity – and when the brain is attacked, repetitious, slurred and confused speech follow. All these things generally happen slowly, so change is hard to recognize if you see a patient regularly. Death can be slow in coming, and people have been known to linger for up to fifteen or twenty years. Bob was of course in a fairly advanced stage, his body was paralysed from the waist down and there was some contraction of the legs, but as yet his arms were comparatively healthy, and thank God his mind was clear; he was however incontinent so that his bed linen and underclothes had constantly to be changed.

As Doreen and I turned him over and lifted him around, I was astonished at her proficiency; she'd learnt the short cuts and I found that far from me helping her, she was teaching me. I felt a bit piqued at this. All right, I'm only five foot and a bit, and I've never practised judo, but I've always fancied myself as a miniature Hercules; my envy was short-lived, after all none of us are too experienced to learn. It wasn't many minutes before a spick-and-span-looking Bob was sitting comfortably in his wheelchair. He'd joked his way through the whole operation and I was reminded of Queen Victoria's remark, quoted so much during the last war, 'In this house we are not interested in the possibility of defeat.'

Doreen gathered up the soiled bed linen and I followed her into the kitchen. I stood there as she began the washing, waiting for her to speak.

She suddenly turned to me, 'I know you're wanting me to tell you all about it. I have nothing to say. I'm most grateful for the help I know you're going to give me, but I don't want to discuss the past, the present or the future.

I've learned to live with what people call "my problem". Talking about it doesn't do any good. I know what's going to happen and so does Bob, let's just leave it at that, and meet each day as it comes.' I nodded in reply, and she turned back to the sink.

'What about the girls?' I asked.

'They've been wonderful, they know all about it too.'

'And money?'

'We manage. National Assistance doesn't allow for any luxuries, but we don't need those now. Mum and Dad aren't short of a bob or two, as you probably know, and they help with the big things.'

I decided that that was enough for my first visit. I thought that bit by bit things would come out to make the picture clearer. Doreen looked well enough and seemed able to cope, it was obvious that she was not one of those people who wanted to bare their souls, though I thought a little sharing of her problems might have helped her. 'I'll see you tomorrow then, around the same time,' I said, and left.

Then followed a series of tomorrows, with no one being quite sure when and where the next blow would fall. The three of us became great friends, all play-acting together. Yet still Doreen remained secretive, she wouldn't share intimacies with me. I tried every way I could to get closer to her, but whenever I seemed to be getting near her she would, as it were, shut the door in my face. But she continued to cope, and cope well.

When I met the children they seemed happy and were helpful, as Doreen had said. I remarked how well dressed they were. 'They make almost all their own clothes, and mainly from other people's cast-offs. We can't afford to have pride these days, and they understand that.' But she did have pride, pride in being able to look after a chronic invalid husband, while still running a house and bringing up a family.

The neighbours too had responded to her courage, as people often will, when they saw the kind of efforts she was making. 'I didn't know we had so many friends,' Doreen said. 'There's a man two doors down who comes and helps me lift and undress Bob, and put him to bed every night. Another, who three times a week wheels him down to the pub; Bob's never been a drinker, but the men there thought he'd enjoy a bit of company, which of course he does. He plays dominoes and crib with them, and if he has any difficulty manipulating things, there's always someone who will help him.' I noticed too that often when I was there a woman would call to collect the day's laundry, after Doreen had washed it. 'She puts it in her spin drier, then irons it for me; she's offered to do the washing but of course I won't let anyone touch Bob's soiled things.' Other neighbours would do the shopping, and every Saturday his brother-in-law came from the farm with a horse box, drawn by a Land-Rover, would wheel Bob's chair into it, and drive him along the coast or around the lakes. If only his illness could have responded to kindness, friendship and good treatment, he would quickly have recovered, and indeed such were his spirits that at times we thought the disease had in fact been halted.

One morning I arrived and was told his left arm had a stiffness in it. Like his legs it quickly locked. A new wheelchair had to be supplied to support it. It wasn't long before the same thing happened to the right arm. But it wasn't what was happening to the arms alone that gave me cause for concern, it was the effect it had on the patient and his family. The play-acting now dwindled, we didn't laugh much any more, and if we did somehow it had a forced, even guilty ring to it. It was now that his GP, Doctor Pringle, arranged an appointment for Bob to see the consultant neurologist. I was there when the ambulance arrived, and helped to get him ready.

The following day I asked Doreen how it had gone. 'I don't want to talk about it,' she said almost rudely. I left it at that, but the next morning brought it up again.

'You must tell me, Doreen, what the specialist said, and what he advises for Bob.'

'Bob,' she replied, 'he doesn't seem particularly interested in him, he told me there was nothing he could do for him. He seemed to think that he should go into hospital, that I was no longer capable of looking after him, and that it would be better for everyone if he went into a ward full of old people, to go to his death in their company.' Doreen was right in one way; if he did go to hospital he would be put in the geriatric ward. 'He said he was thinking of me and the children. Indeed he was more interested in me than Bob. I don't know how to tell you, nurse, but he became most personal, asking questions that have nothing whatsoever to do with him, or with Bob. Questions about my sex life. He made me feel dirty inside. And there were two nurses in the room at the time. I'll never see that man again, never.'

She put her hands to her face and I expected to see her break down and cry for the first time. I almost hoped she would, but when she lowered them her face was set.

'Don't let's ever talk about that visit again,' she said.

I did of course bring it up later, and tried to explain that the consultant's questions were not out of curiosity, but from concern; she wouldn't have it, it was like talking to a wall. I now wondered whether Doreen's attitude was one of courage, or of obstinacy.

Like the neurologist, I began to regard her as my patient more than Bob, my eyes went first to her on my daily visits. I tried casting my mind back over the last twelve months recalling the bright, red-cheeked woman I had met when I'd first started my regular calls, and as I looked at her now it became obvious that the strain had taken its toll. Her hair had rapidly become grey, her eyes sunken, and the colour in her cheeks was now streaky. Then came the first of the physical manifestations; she developed a stye on one eye, it was slow to heal and was followed by others; boils appeared under her arms and on her legs. I suggested that she saw Doctor Pringle. 'I'm not mithering the life out of him with my small ailments, he's got enough to do in this house looking after Bob.' Eventually the doctor examined her, but she gave him short shrift, and if she did go to the chemist with the prescription he gave, I don't believe she ever took what was prescribed; it was as if she'd taken against the medical profession as a result of her visit to the neurologist.

The disease progressed as we knew it had to, and eventually Bob's brain cells began to degenerate and his speech became so slurred as to become incomprehensible. It was slow, insidious and almost imperceptible in the way it happened, which made it, if anything, worse for us who could only stand by, watch and wait. It was now that I noticed a change in the children, and particularly in Mary, who was the elder of the two. She had become aggressive, constantly at odds with her mother, treating the house just as somewhere to eat and sleep, and for my taste at any rate, was using too much make-up and seemed to be flaunting herself. I knew it was something I couldn't remark on to Doreen, and of course she was too proud to discuss her family, even with the friend that I had now become. I found myself in a dilemma. If, as common sense dictated, I put the full case to the medical authorities they would, I knew, coerce Doreen into putting Bob into hospital. It would have relieved much of the pressure on her. But then I thought, what effect would this have? She had set herself the task of looking after Bob to the end. It had become her life's purpose, an obsession if you like, but was it right to deny her the opportunity of fulfilling it, and what would be her reaction if it was forced upon her?

Thoughts like these were now constantly going through my mind. One morning came a summons from Mrs Mac. There was no hesitation in her manner at this meeting.

'Nurse, ah'm taking you off the Saunders case. It's not them ah'm thinking aboot,' she said, 'it's ye. It's evident that ye've got yourself too involved emotionally. It was a thing ah tried to warn ye not to do. It's obvious to everyone around that ye're not yourself, and if you go on behaving as ye are ye'll fall ill and be of no good to anybody.'

To some extent she was right, of course, but I was determined to fight my corner. It took me a good quarter of an hour to make Mrs Mac change her mind. That I got a qualified reprieve was an achievement I think. I won it when I said, 'It's easy for doctors and hospital nurses to bridle their feelings, but surely with district nurses it's different. In a case like this, involvement is inevitable if not absolutely necessary.'

As things turned out, I wasn't to have much longer on the case. Early one morning my phone rang, and on the other end was the Saunders' daughter Mary, sounding very frightened.

'Nurse, will you please come at once.'

'Why, what's the matter?' I asked.

'It's our mum.'

I didn't bother to find out details, I was dressed and in my car in a matter of minutes. A crying Mary opened the door to me. 'She's upstairs in bed.' I didn't wait for explanations. The bedroom floor was strewn with soaking wet clothes, and Doreen was shivering and sobbing into the pillow.

'What's been going on?' I asked almost roughly. She buried her face further into the pillow. I was familiar enough with this sort of situation to know what to do. I stood back from the bed and shouted, 'Pull yourself together – feeling sorry for yourself isn't going to do anyone any good. Tell me, what has happened?' It did the trick. She lifted herself up in the bed and put her arms out towards me. I moved to her, we sat there clasped together, and gradually the story came tumbling out:

'Yesterday was terrible – every day lately seems to have got worse – but then Bob was particularly tiresome. Oh I know he doesn't mean to be – I know it's not his fault – but there seems to be no sense in him – he's not the man I married any more, Pat – I feel as though all the love I had for him has left me – it hasn't of course, but recently it seems like that. Then Mary and I had a blazing row – the worst yet – she was out till midnight and I'm frightened for her, but the more I try and tell her, the worse it all gets – she said last night she was leaving home for good – she couldn't stand it here any more, and I told her to get out. I came to bed and tried to sleep – I need sleep – I haven't had a proper night's rest for weeks. Then it all started drilling into my mind – I knew I'd failed, and it had been my whole life's dream to succeed – it seemed to me there was no longer any purpose in life, no point in going on trying – I got up, dressed and walked down to the seafront – it was a quiet night and it looked so peaceful – I wandered on to the sand. And then I walked into the sea.

'It didn't seem cold – I felt as though it welcomed me. When the water was up to my waist, I turned to have what I thought was my last look at the land, and it was then that I realized what I was doing. I screamed and swore at the sea as I stumbled back to the shore – then I ran home. I must have made a noise getting into the house, because Mary woke and came to my room – and that's why you're here now.'

Other intimacies and confidences came tumbling out, and at last I got the complete picture of what life had been like for her over the past years. Eventually I felt she was sufficiently relaxed and comforted for me to leave her. I had a quick word or two with Mary, to ease her mind, for she seemed to think it had all been her fault, and was almost as shocked and depressed as her mother. I told her to make some hot drinks for us all. Bob, I'm glad to say, had slept through the whole drama, not poor love that if he had been awake he would have known what it was all about. I then phoned Doctor Pringle, and explained something of what had happened; he'd just started his surgery. 'I'll soon get rid of them, nurse, and I'll be right over.' His patients couldn't have known what hit them that morning, for we'd hardly finished our drinks when the doorbell went, and he was there with us.

I sent Mary up to her mother while I told him the full story.

'In a way it's a God-sent situation, nurse, even though it has been a near tragic one. Mrs Saunders is a stubborn woman, though I wish I had more patients like her – willing to try to shoulder a few of life's burdens, rather than passing them on to other people.'

He went upstairs. I knew what he was going to do – explain to Doreen that now was the time when Bob must go into hospital, that she'd finally proved to herself, and everyone else, that she was no longer able to do any more for him, and that if she continued to try, it would be at the expense of her daughters' future, and her own health. He took his time. After about half an hour he called Mary in, and through the emotion of the moment, was able to bring about a reconciliation between mother and daughter.

'The rest is up to you, nurse,' he said to me, when he came downstairs and handed me a prescription for Doreen. 'I don't think you'll find it difficult.'

There was something in his tone that made me look at him more closely. This was a different Doctor Pringle from the dour, ascetic practitioner I was accustomed to. He turned away to avoid my stare, and walking to the front door he took his handkerchief from his pocket and blew his nose.

It was then that I wished Mrs Mac could have seen

him. She would have had proof that it wasn't only nurses who got emotionally involved with their patients.

Bob lived for two years after he went into hospital, with Doreen and her family visiting him regularly. Later both of her daughters married, and she returned to her father's farm to live a useful and happy life.

Chapter Eleven

The practice of medicine, like farming, often used to run in the family. I say used to, because today young people seem to want to break away from their parents' control, even their influence. They prefer to do their own thing, in their own way and on their own. Doctor Wilfred Cooper's two sons however conformed to the traditional pattern, and not only followed their father's profession, but when they had qualified joined his practice as junior partners. Their parents couldn't have anticipated this, it seemed, for at their christenings they were both given the initial 'W', the same as their father's. The first son was Walter, and to confuse the issue still further, the second was called Wilfred, after his father. This particular difficulty of identification was got over by patients and nurses alike, who referred to them as old Doctor Wilf, and young Doctor Wilf, so in that way mistakes were rarely made.

One thing distinguished old Wilf from his two sons, his handwriting was legible, while they seemed to vie with each other with their unintelligible scribble. They were the despair of the local chemists, who occasionally handed prescriptions back to patients, and when they protested at the delay this would cause, offered to prepare them at their own risk: 'It's up to you. I'll have a guess at it, but you must choose whether you would rather be cured than killed.' It was rumoured that one pharmacist returned the prescription saying that it was a receipt from the Chinese laundry. The patient took it there and got three shirts in exchange!

Another thing that set the old doctor apart from his boys was his treatments, which were of the good old-fashioned, no-nonsense type. Patients suffering from chest conditions were prescribed twice-daily applications of kaolin poultices. For aching backs or rheumatism sufferers he ordered mustard plasters and strong smelling rubefacients. Mothers not wishing to breast-feed their babies, and who were enduring agony from their enlarged mammary glands, took small relief from his prescribed doses of Epsom salts.

His two sons, and in particular young Wilf, who had only recently qualified, didn't approve of these primitive methods, yet both managed to introduce their up-to-date treatments without causing their father any distress or embarrassment. As is generally the habit in family practices, all three visited each others' patients, so that when one of the sons went to a patient who was being treated with kaolin poultices, he would leave a message for the district nurse, prescribing antibiotic injections, yet emphasizing that the poultice treatment must be continued. Mothers suffering from engorged breasts, were given either an injection of testosterone (the male hormone), or a course of stilboestrol tablets (this method of scaling milk is not used today), yet doses of Epsom salts would be continued. Rheumatic patients were ordered Butozolo-dine, but the painful joints would still have to be rubbed with rubefacients or embrocation, as Doctor Cooper called them.

The result was that everyone was happy, the Coopers and their patients, particularly the older ones, who suffered the young doctors' treatments, but would say that it was the old doctor who was responsible for the easing of their pain. 'Them young'ns have a lot to learn from t' gov'ner yet.'

The Coopers were regular visitors to Heathfield Hall. Old Doctor Cooper was a widower. He dressed in the traditional manner, black jacket and striped trousers, though giving the impression that he would have preferred wearing a morning coat. He was a friendly man, with a gentle face and voice, who seemed to seek the society of women. He would talk by the hour to the nurses of the good old days, when he cycled to visit his patients, and of the thrill of his first motorbike. He spoke almost wistfully of rickets, tuberculosis, diphtheria, scarlet and typhoid fever, and the havoc these diseases had caused when they struck the community, and the work they gave to the doctors. He spoke too of the gratitude patients showed in those days, and their easier acceptance of pain and death. He gave the impression that suffering somehow ennobled, and though he applauded the miracles of modern science, he felt that it had in some way destroyed the soul. 'If only we could turn the clock back fifty years, just for one week, Patricia, perhaps people would realize how lucky they are today,' he would sigh.

Walter Cooper was a tall, lanky, fair-haired man of around thirty-six, when I joined the service. Although he'd been away at school and later at a teaching hospital, he remained very much a local boy with roots firmly fixed in Burrowdale. He knew about the conditions in the shipyards and of local industry, so quickly found a talking point with those he treated. He would break into the vernacular, if he thought it helped to put a patient at ease. His wife Elizabeth was the daughter of one of the wealthier shop owners of the town, and like her husband, was very much a Burrowdale local. She adored children, and proved it by having six of her own. She also devoted herself to Walter's work, took a real interest in his patients, and received and delivered messages with accuracy and charm. She was loved by all the nurses. 'Busty', who was critical of any relationship, couldn't fault her, even though she fancied her husband, and said so.

'Busty's' prime target however was young Wilf Cooper, and she used every trick she knew to seduce him, but the harder she tried the more aloof he became. The situation was embarrassing for everyone around, and eventually we told her so. This cooled her a bit, but it wasn't until he announced that he had a fiancée in London, that she finally gave up. When we heard of this attachment, some of us were afraid that 'Busty' would turn on the 'Hell hath no fury' stuff, that was so much part of her. She didn't, but her attitude to Wilf changed. Instead of the seductress, she became the teaser, playing on his youth and shyness. 'How's your Helen getting on? Behaving herself I hope, in the big city,' she would say as though doubting that this was possible. Once when he returned from a weekend in London she began, 'Did you have a good time, Wilfred?'

'Yes, rather,' he replied enthusiastically.

'Where did you go?'

'Well, we didn't exactly go anywhere.'

'Oh, didn't you, then what did you do?'

'Well, we didn't actually do anything,' he replied lamely.

'Now that sounds like what I'd call a wonderfully romantic weekend,' and Doctor Wilf's blushes indicated that he got her message. Once she managed to get him to show her some photos of Helen, 'Mm, very dishy, but I wonder what kind of a doctor's wife she'll make.'

It wasn't long after their marriage that 'Busty's' implied forebodings were shown to be true. Helen was in absolute contrast to her homely sister-in-law. She was tall, shapely, and by Burrowdale's standards, highly sophisticated, which means that we didn't understand most of what she was saying. She dressed expensively, and always in the fashion. She was over-confident to the point of rudeness, and by her disparaging references to the town and its inhabitants she made it plain that she was bored to distraction. It was natural, therefore, that we should react to her as she did to us, and Northern contempt is not an easy thing to live with.

She did try to be a doctors' wife, by taking messages and phone calls, and passing them on where necessary. Unfortunately, with her temperament and manner, the results were disastrous. She began by antagonizing the district nurses. She would telephone her husband's requests as though they were her personal orders, 'This is Mrs Wilfred Cooper here, I want a district nurse to go to . . .' as though she was speaking to some unknown subordinate. She completely monopolized the telephone, so a nurse ringing young Doctor Wilf almost invariably had to speak to her. Give her her due, I expect she was trying to protect her husband, but for a nurse who was asking for advice to be told that 'You must know what the doctor usually does under such circumstances, so I suggest you do it,' was infuriating, and very unprofessional. I tried baffling her with science, by using jaw-breaking medical terms to describe even the most minor ailments. If a patient was running a temperature I would describe him as pyrexial, and tachycardial if his pulse was rapid. It didn't help, she demanded explanations, at the same time writing the words down, remembering them and using them later to everyone's disadvantage.

The time came when she was to give proof to the saying,

'A little learning is a dangerous thing'. Anne Evans, the colleague who had given me my earlier introduction into the world of the district nurse, was privileged to administer the *coup de grâce*. This was only fair, as Helen's behaviour offended her deep sense of ethics more than anyone else's. Anne had in her care a new mother, suffering from a breast abscess. She'd noticed that her baby was snuffly, and overnight it developed a sticky eye. She phoned young Doctor Wilf, Helen answered and after informing Anne that the doctor was too busy to be disturbed, she demanded to be told the details of the case. Anne smoothly and accurately gave them.

'From what you have told me, it would seem obvious that the child is teething,' was Helen's quick diagnosis.

'If he is then he will have made medical history, by being the first baby of fourteen days to do so,' was Anne's frosty comment.

One would have thought that now Helen would have proceeded cautiously; instead she lost her temper and directed Anne to bathe the baby's eye with a boracic solution. Anne, realizing that she had the fish on the line, decided to play it.

'It's your opinion that your husband would prescribe that?'

'Yes, of course, I know he would,' said the voice of inexperience firmly and forcibly. With a quick 'Thank you very much' Anne rang off. She knew it was a procedure that had had disastrous results over the country. She was not being personally vindictive when she reported the matter to Mrs Mac, for she had consulted a few of us first, and we were all agreed that since Helen might be advising patients to do the same thing, it was time that she was stopped.

Mrs Mac's reaction was predictable; she was delighted. 'It's time that fliperty-jiberty, stuck-up Sassenach was given a lesson,' she cried, as she picked up the phone and asked old Doctor Cooper to step around and see her as soon as possible. 'It's verrry urgent,' she said, and from the way she rolled her 'Rs' he must have thought it critical, for he was round in minutes.

We all believed that Mrs Mac was hoping for a show-down with Helen, but Doctor Wilf was a downy old bird, and on this occasion as tactful with his son as he had been to him. There was no confrontation: he changed the system, appointed a receptionist, and it was through her that all messages were passed from then on. Young Doctor Wilf found a cure for Helen's possible boredom, for she speedily became pregnant.

I only had one major battle with Helen during her early initiation period as a doctor's wife. While I was nursing Bob Saunders at Seaspray, it was suggested by Evelyn Telford that as I was going there daily, I should take over the case of young Tony Squire.

Tony was what we called at that time a 'ton-up' boy, a kind of forerunner to the Hell's Angels, though without their unsavoury reputation. He'd been thrown from his motorbike by an overtaking car, which had driven him into the side of the road, some six months before I met him. He had been lucky to escape with his life, but from the way he described his 'smashing smash-up' it sounded as though he'd enjoyed the experience. He had got away with nothing more than a fractured femur; then his luck failed him, he developed osteomyelitis – an inflammation of the bone and marrow – due to an infection in the bloodstream, which was probably caused at the time of the accident. It meant that the broken bone would not heal easily, and that it might take up to two years to mend. Tony, of course, was not told how long it might take. To a nineteen-year-old boy, two years can seem a very long time.

From the day that I first visited him it was apparent that Tony would provide the light relief I needed from the growing tensions of Bob Saunders. He was a happy, devil-may-care boy, who could squeeze fun out of any situation. Nothing, it seemed, worried him. If anything, his accident had increased his enthusiasm for the motorbike. The walls of his bedroom were evidence of this; they were covered with posters and pin-ups of the bikes and great riders of the time. These gradually gave way to pictures of nurses from 'Emergency Ward Ten', the television programme, but pride of place at his bedside was given to a photograph of a pretty trainee nurse. I must disclaim all responsibility for this obsession of his, it had nothing to do with our relationship. During his time in hospital, it seemed he had fallen head over heels in love with a probationer, and his affection had been returned. 'She's going to be a "real" nurse,' was the unintentionally hurtful remark he made to me once. He was not alone in this kind of thinking, a number of other patients considered district nurses in this way, and said so. At first it made me indignant, and I tried to explain their misapprehensions away; eventually I let my experience speak for itself.

Tony lived with his grandparents in the old village school, which had been converted into a large bungalow and made a delightful home for them. One of the classrooms had been turned into a conservatory, and the glass extension at the back gave a perfect view of the little fishing and yachting harbour. The garden had been planned with the expertise and care of a landscape gardener. Perhaps his surroundings were responsible for Tony's high spirits, for no one could have wanted a better place in which to convalesce. He was completely spoiled by his grandparents, who seemed to dote on him. The Squires were not, as I'd originally thought, Tony's father's parents, but his mother's; so I was curious to get to know something about his background.

Mr Squire was an executive in the shipyards, a member of the village council and on the committee of the local yacht club; a busy, florid-faced little man, with a cheerful outgoing disposition. He was a bad listener, constantly interrupting with, 'If I may say so,' and then dogmatically doing just that. Mrs Squire was a quiet agreeing woman, to the point of irritation, 'Yes nurse, of course nurse, I'll see that it's done nurse.' She never queried any requests that I made, nor did she ask for any explanations. Her appearance mirrored her personality; she wore what I call careful clothes, that is, clothes that no one could fault. They were well and expensively made, but registered nothing. Even the hats, which she wore constantly, giving the impression that she was either coming or going, all seemed alike. The love and affection for their grandson seemed to be the only thing they had in common, yet their lives fitted easily together. It was apparent that Tony was illegitimate; and the moment I mentioned his parents, everyone closed up like a clam.

I decided that I would just accept the situation, and enjoy treating their happy-go-lucky grandson. After a couple of months Tony developed some minor infection in his wound, and I thought it best to ring young Doctor Wilf for advice. As usual I only got as far as Helen. I began explaining why I had phoned. I had got half way through my report when she broke in angrily, 'The boy has no right to expect any treatment. He's one of those damn menaces that make life dangerous for everyone on the roads. I don't see why my husband's precious time has to be wasted on him. The first thing he'll do when he's well again is to smash himself up and probably someone else too,' and so it went on.

'Mrs Cooper,' I eventually interrupted, 'it's not my place to decide on the ethics of this case. It's my duty to heal the sick, and if the boy was a murderer I would still do everything in my power to get him back to health. I know that your husband would do the same, so will you please ask him to get in touch with me as soon as possible.'

She then became almost hysterical, 'You medical people are all the same, you make me sick.'

'The cure is in your hands,' I retorted. 'Keep away from us, and don't try to interfere with something you know little about.'

When Doctor Wilf phoned me, I expected some sort of rebuke for my directness, which to Helen would have appeared as rudeness, but from his manner towards me I don't think she could have told him about it. When I next spoke to her she was almost friendly, and I thought perhaps I had persuaded her to mend her ways. I'm afraid it was a conceit on my part, for she gave us only a short respite, and within a few days she was back in the saddle, riding her high horse once again.

The business of district nursing I had found to be one of give and take. There are few patients that I've looked after who haven't contributed something to my life. From Tony's descriptions I learned how to ride a motorbike without ever having to get on a machine, which was just as well because, like Helen, I was frightened of them, and hated the wretched things. Unlike Helen, however, I believed every one of us has the right to make a personal choice, and during my life I have resented the way these freedoms are being taken away from us. By the very nature of my job, the preservation of life is of the greatest importance to me, but those who get enjoyment from putting their lives to risk should not, I believe, be restrained. Courage, like any other quality, needs to be nurtured and put to the test in health as well as in sickness, so when accidents occur as a result, I am prepared to give my time and experience willingly to mend broken bodies.

Tony's other obsession was pop music, which was something I knew little about when I first visited him, but by the end of his treatment he was able to announce to his grandparents that Nurse Pat was 'with it', and part of the scene. If he had had his way he would have had me out of 'all that clobber', as he described my uniform; he said I'd look better mini-skirted and in kinky boots, with a shining black leather jacket to keep me warm in the winter.

I couldn't understand his antipathy towards my uniform in view of his infatuation with the student nurse, Millicent, 'my Millie', as he referred to her. He told me he thought her 'rig' was way out, with all that starch and those Batman cloaks. His affection for her stood the test of time, which was extraordinary, since I would have thought that even the most ardent of lovers would have been restrained by a broken and infected femur. Not Tony, he worked out a system whereby he could visit the hospital at Burrowdale regularly once a fortnight. He would tell either his grandparents or me that he had an appointment with the orthopaedic consultant there, but that the card confirming this had not arrived. One of us would ring through to the hospital, and the clerk there, after searching in vain through the files and unable to discover evidence of it, would cover herself by making an appointment, assuming naturally that no one would want to go to hospital unnecessarily. Tony in the meantime had made a date with Millicent, and they would spend an hour or two in the waiting room, holding hands and whispering to each other. It was many weeks before we discovered his cunning, and I'm glad to say it was treated as a great joke by all concerned. The discovery also helped the young lovers, for Tony's grandparents, who previously had refused to take his passion seriously and so had not encouraged her to visit him, now decided that rather than break his heart, she would be welcome at any time.

It wasn't until I had been nursing Tony for some months that I uncovered the mystery that surrounded his parents. One day when I called at the house the door was answered by a distressed-looking Mrs Squire, who was holding a handkerchief to her eyes. 'Can I have a word with you, nurse, before you see Tony?' We went into the sitting room. I sat down opposite her and she removed the handkerchief, revealing swollen and bloodshot eyes. She then began her story.

'Before I went to bed, my eyes began to hurt, and during the night my eyelids have swollen and they're now discharging.'

I was about to break in and say it looked and sounded like a severe attack of conjunctivitis, but she stopped me.

'There's something I want you to know, nurse. I have

every reason to be worried about my eyes, and I must tell you why. Our daughter, Tony's mother, when she was about Tony's age, suffered what I think might have been a similar attack, and eventually became blind in both eyes. She went to an institution to learn to live with her disability. We visited her regularly, and she seemed to be getting on well and we were looking forward to having her back home with us. Then one day she told us she was pregnant. As you can imagine we were very shaken, though after we had had time to think it over, Mr Squire and I were able to accept it, and we told her so, and that we would be glad to have them both at home with us. She wouldn't hear of this, and insisted that the child must be adopted. The father, you see, refused to have anything more to do with her, and she felt she couldn't face the world, both blind and with an illegitimate child. We didn't know now what to do, whether to agree to the baby being adopted and bringing our daughter home, or whether to keep our grandchild and bring him up, leaving Mary in the institute. Mary made our decision easier by the way she behaved. She was almost fiendish towards her child; when Tony was born she refused to feed him, or even handle him. She seemed half mad and we saw that if she returned home, she would make our lives difficult, if not impossible to endure. So rightly or wrongly we chose Tony. We moved here almost immediately after he joined us, so that we could make a new life and escape the judgement of our friends and neighbours. The reason I have told you all this is that Mr Squire and I have always had the dread that Mary's blindness might have been due to some hereditary weakness, and that some day one of us might be attacked in the same way. Would you therefore be kind enough to have a look at my eyes, and give me your opinion as to what I should do?'

I was astounded, not only at the story she had told me, but that she should ask for my diagnosis on a matter that was of such importance and concern to her. I told her this, and suggested that she saw Doctor Cooper right away. 'But won't you just look at them now, and tell me what you think?' she almost beseeched me. Then I realized how her mind was working. It was something I'd come across most frequently with women who had developed lumps in their breasts. They were alarmed thinking that it might be a cancer, but the dread of discovering that it was made them postpone seeing their doctor. They would rather live with their anxiety than face the confirmation of their worst fears. I don't think I need comment on this way of thinking.

Since I was almost sure that Mrs Squire was suffering from nothing more than conjunctivitis, I did examine her, suggested that she should bathe her eyes in warm, sterile water and advised her to take certain other precautions, so that the complaint didn't spread to other members of the family; at the same time I made her promise to see Doctor Cooper as soon as possible. I'm glad to say that as I thought it was all a storm in a teacup, though Mrs

Squire's story was something I pondered over for some time. There's no doubt that the solution they'd chosen for their problem had given them an uncomplicated life, but I wondered what the daughter had been able to make of hers, and what Tony's future reaction might be to their decision.

Of course when Tony's leg eventually healed my visits ceased, but he did phone me not long afterwards to invite me to his engagement party. He and his Nurse Millie had come to an understanding. There was to be no wedding in the immediate future, she was going to finish her training first, but both of them felt more secure with a marriage to look forward to. It was a rather self-conscious sort of gathering, with parents and grandparents trying desperately hard to like each other, and to accept a situation about which both parties were unsure. There was however a happy climax at the end. As a gift for Tony, the Squires had bought him a brand new motorbike. It was drawn up outside and we gathered around for the presentation. Tony's face lit up when he saw it, he fondled it with his eyes and then with his hands. I wondered, a trifle cynically, which of his loves was the greater. Excitedly he grabbed Millie and together they dashed indoors, to reappear in leather jackets. They jumped on to the machine, a kick start from Tony and they were away up into the hills, with the guests cheering them as they disappeared from sight.

As I was going back into the house, two villagers passed by. 'There ought to be a law against it,' one remarked. The other took up the theme, 'Bluddy young fool is yon. 'e's already near killed 'is self. Trouble with young lads today, they won't be towd.'

'You two should get together with Helen,' I said to myself, though at that moment I had butterflies in my stomach for the Tony I had helped to mend, and his pretty young nurse.

Chapter Twelve

The National Health Service was like the other government services in that as it developed those of us in the fighting line soon found there were too many chiefs and too few Indians. Doctors and nurses alike were overloaded with work, while administrators, with little to do, exercised themselves by pulling out the drawers of their desks, then pushing them back with their stomachs, so developing strong and healthy muscles. It doesn't take long to train an administrator. Unfortunately, it takes seven years to qualify as a doctor, and a minimum of three to become a state registered nurse. Even so, when the shortage of Indians became acute, it was considered that steps had to be taken to try to fill the ranks.

Nothing much could be done for the doctors, except to continue to exhort them to keep at it, but to lighten the load for nurses it was decided that we should recruit what were called nursing auxiliaries. It was a high-sounding title, but titles, as we have learned over the years, mean little unless they are earned by merit and ability. All right, we could see how these auxiliaries could be helpful in hospitals relieving nurses of repetitive jobs like cleaning lockers, serving meals, changing water jugs, making empty beds and looking after the flowers, but since district nurses were mostly involved with tending chronically ill patients and the elderly, we were unable to imagine how they could be of any use to us. Time has to a great extent proved that we were wrong. Nurses and indeed the medical profession as a whole dislike changes of routine and oppose them whenever they are suggested. We also knew that in the beginning we would have to teach the auxiliaries and we were unsure as to how far this teaching would have to go. We knew though that, far from helping us during their training, they would be a hindrance, so we determined to resist them. We were also unfortunate with our initial intake.

I remember the day when the news came through that we were shortly to receive three auxiliary recruits. It was one of Mrs Mac's black days. She was quick to realize what it would mean, and came bounding into the nurses' sitting room to tell us.

'It makes a mockery of the service,' she declared. 'Ah've spent my life preserving the principles for which we stand, and now some government ignoramus destroys them in one fell swoop. "Ease our work load" it says here,' and she waved a letter in our faces. 'It'll double it, that's what it'll do. Well, all I can say is that these' – she looked at the letter again – '*auxiliaries*' – the way she pronounced it made them sound like the scum of the earth – 'will have to work their fingers to the bone to earn their trumped-up title here.'

With that she stormed out of the room.

I suppose I should have guessed what her attitude would be, when three weeks later we were assembled to meet three self-conscious and bewildered-looking recruits, who hovered near the door, trying hard to pretend they were not there. Mrs Mac relished any occasion when she was called on to make a speech. She thrived on an audience, particularly one on whom she could work to create an impression of authority and efficiency. She referred to the district nursing service of Burrowdale as 'my team', and spoke of the high traditions of the service, which must never be allowed to deteriorate. Although she must have delivered this speech fifty times, in my experience, she continually glanced at her notes, which were fastened to a board by an ugly looking bulldog clip, as if they gave her inspiration. Indeed this piece of equipment was as much a part of her as her frizzy grey hair, rimless spectacles and booming Scottish voice.

Eventually, with the hackneyed bit over, we knew she would have to speak about the auxiliaries, and because of her earlier attitude, we all wondered what she would have to say. She glanced down at her board. 'Now, team, ah'm sure you will join me in welcoming these ladies into our ranks, and that you will do everything in your power to help them in their early days, confident in the thought that shortly they will be helping you in your duties.' I felt eleven other bodies around me stiffen as mine did, and heard 'Busty's' 'hypocritical bitch', whispered through clenched teeth. There were no 'hear hear's' or welcome noises from 'the team'. I looked at the newcomers smiling nervously from pink faces. Mrs Mac then went on to say how she proposed to dispose them. 'Ye will each be attached to a district nurse for a period of four weeks. That will mean that by the end of yer first year, ye will have had the benefit of the experience of everyone here.' Then she read out the names of those of the nurses with whom they were to begin their work. I was relieved that mine was not among them, it meant that I had time to learn from the experiences of my colleagues. 'Busty' was not so fortunate, and when her name was linked with that of Mrs Ada Tyson, she responded with a nod and a very short word.

'Busty's' Ada, as we referred to her during that first month, was a big, gaunt woman, with gangling arms and long skinny legs, well into her middle forties. When speaking, she had the habit of throwing her arms over her head and clapping them together, to give force to a particular statement; she would do the same if she happened to see the point of a joke, which was usually a minute after it had been told. At such moments she looked for all the world like a praying mantis. She was also given to malapropisms, with remarks like, 'Ee, it's a reet shame about them boys being 'eld ostriches in Africa.' Nor did she show early promise as a nurse when she announced, 'Me owd fellar were up all neet. 'e 'ad that gastric stummack comin' on 'im again. 'e won't be towd, yer know.'

Nevertheless Ada helped cheer our lives, for if we inquired of 'Busty', 'How's your Ada getting on?' we were treated to both humour and invective. Ada couldn't drive, so 'Busty' was an 'unpaid chauffeur' – picking her up and taking her home. 'She's not even grateful, she keeps telling me there's not enough room in the car for her feet. Of course there bloody isn't, she takes size twelves. When she lifts patients, she holds them in a half-nelson. I have to keep telling her to lift them, not strangle them.' In this way we got a blow by blow commentary on Ada's progress.

The climax came; it was fortunate for Ada that it was at the end of her first training period. 'Busty' had in her care an old spinster lady, Mary Ellis, who suffered from a rectal prolapse. I think if I describe it in medical terms it will give an idea what it's like. It's the protrusion of the mucous membrane, and sometimes of the muscle coat as well, through the anal canal to the exterior. It isn't a pleasant thing to look at, or to have to treat by constantly replacing the offending part; nor of course to suffer, though Miss Ellis had learnt to live with it and couldn't understand what all the fuss was about. 'It don't bother me none, luv, why don't you leave it be?' I think 'Busty' would have been prepared to do this if Miss Ellis hadn't been Doctor Rankin's patient; she was acting under his instructions, and he always insisted that these were carried out to the letter.

When 'Busty' had first introduced Ada to Miss Ellis's anal prolapse, she greeted it with a shudder, and a 'Ee, what a nasty sight.' This unprofessional remark didn't please the old lady. 'I don't 'spose your bum's much to look at either,' she said indignantly. 'Busty' managed to restore the peace, though later she tore the unfortunate Ada off a strip. On another visit it was found that Doctor Rankin had written on the report sheet, which served as a liaison between doctor and nurse, that some sort of bandage should be prepared to try to keep the offending part in its rightful position. After reading it 'Busty' was in difficulty trying to determine the right kind of bandage to use. Suddenly she had an inspiration. 'Come along with me,' she commanded Ada, 'I know the very thing that'll do the trick.' Together they drove to the out-patients department at the local hospital, where they met the nursing sister, a prissy woman, who spoke with a plum in her mouth. She took a scathing look at gawky Ada, then turned to 'Busty'.

'Ken eye be of assistance?' she inquired.

'I hope so,' 'Busty' replied. 'I want six scrotal suspensory bandages.'

'Eye big your pardin, what did you say?'

'Ball bags for the ball bags,' said 'Busty' coarsely. 'Things for men, have you got any?'

'Eye reely think you should be more careful of your lenguage,' the sister looked round cautiously. 'Eye think eye know what you mean. Eye'll go and have a look.'

She returned with the required articles, and 'Busty'

quickly left with a bewildered Ada on her heels, and returned to her patient. She then fitted the bandage around the offending area, and feeling rather pleased with her handiwork left to continue her rounds.

'Do you think you can manage to do that next time?' she asked Ada as they drove away.

'Aye, I think ah'll manage.'

'Well, you're going to have to try, you can only learn by doing.'

True to her word, when the time came for the next visit to Miss Ellis, 'Busty' dropped her at the door. 'You're on your own now. Good luck, I'll be back in half an hour.' Then, as an afterthought, she added, 'Don't forget to fill in the report sheet.' When she returned to collect her auxiliary, she found a confident Ada, well pleased with her recent performance. 'It 'ad slipped out again, but ah've tucked it back. Let's 'ope it stays in this time.'

'Did you do the report?'

'Aye, that's OK.'

Two days later 'Busty' was in the nurses' sitting room, getting ready to go home, when in burst an angry-looking Doctor Rankin.

'Nurse Clarke, I believe you are looking after Miss Ellis, are you not?' he demanded through tight lips.

'Yes, doctor, I am,' replied 'Busty'.

'It seems you have an exaggerated sense of humour, and in the worst possible taste,' he said as he handed her the buff-coloured envelope containing the report sheet. 'You will fill that in properly, and don't ever try to be funny at a patient's expense again.'

He turned and walked out of the room. 'Busty' opened the envelope and looked at the report. It was the one Ada had written.

'Miss Ellis's scrotum keeps collapsing.'

I'm happy to say I never had to contend with Ada's services. Her next attachment was to Anne Evans, the super-perfectionist. Within a week Mrs Mac was presented with an ultimatum, 'Either she goes or I do'; our superintendent had no option.

It was three months after the scheme had been initiated that my turn came, and I was told that I was to have the help of a Mrs Marjorie May, or 'Daisy' May, as she had been christened by Chrissie Brooks, the nurse to whom she was first attached, because of an irritating habit she had when lifting a patient of saying, 'Oopsy daisy.' Daisy was a rotund little woman, a widow of about forty, with bleached platinum blonde hair, and a mincingly officious manner. The reports I had had of her were not encouraging. Chrissie was a kind and tolerant person, so her faint praise was damning, 'I suppose she means well, and she's keen as mustard, but she doesn't seem able to listen, and thinks she knows it all. And she's full of her own importance, sometimes I think the patients wonder who's the nurse and who's the auxiliary. The way she pronounces the word "auxiliary" makes a lot of them think it's some kind of high rank. Still never mind what I say, I'm sure you two will get on.'

Diane Metcalf, who took Daisy over from Chrissie, was not so charitable. She described her as an occupational hazard and a menace to the service. 'If ever she tells me again that although I'm the one with the letters after my name, she is the one with experience, and that experience is the best teacher, so help me I'll strangle her. What I'm trying to find out is where she got what she calls her experience. Then she has the effrontery to call doctors by their Christian names. Wilf, for old Doctor Cooper, and Hugh for Doctor Morton. "My late husband and I knew them socially you know",' Diane mimicked.

I had the opportunity of hearing Diane's criticism confirmed. A few of us were sitting around in the nurses' common room, Daisy was chatting away to the ever-patient Chrissie Brooks, with Diane hovering around the magazine table. I think Daisy was directing this particular bit of conversation at Diane, for raising her voice she said, 'As dear old Wilf told me just before my husband died, "Nurses are born, not made, Marjorie, and it's my opinion you have the calling."' Whether she was intended to hear it or not, Diane came in smartly with, 'Yes, but what Doctor Cooper forgot to add was, that while many are called, few are chosen.' With the laughter that followed there was nothing Daisy could do but leave the room as quickly as she could.

I think both Diane and Daisy must have heaved sighs of

relief when it came to my turn to take over. For my part, I breathed a sigh of resignation, though by the evening of just one day with her that resignation had changed to indignation.

My first three calls were on diabetic patients, who needed only insulin injections. They were well supplied with syringes, needles, urine-testing equipment and their life-saving drug, insulin, so there was no need to take anything into their homes. I knew that Daisy must have been in attendance on many diabetic patients already, so I was astonished when stopping at the first house I saw her dive into the back of the car to grab my nursing bag. I told her it was completely unnecessary, yet she ignored me and strutting off through the gate and up the garden path, she pushed the front door open and cried, 'Cooee, it's only me, the district nurse.'

The pattern continued. By the end of the third injection I was left wondering exactly who I was supposed to be. By the end of the day I was reeling. Most of my patients had formed their opinions of my officious aid: 'Ah tak it you're a sort of matron, and you've come along to see that the nurse does her job, proper like' was a typical remark which Daisy brightly side-stepped, 'Well, not quite, I'm here to help you get well again.'

When I got home that evening, my husband Colin noticed that there was something wrong with me, 'What's the matter, luv, you don't seem your usual self.'

'What self? I don't think I have a self any more,' and

then I described the events of the day. It was a pity that he had to laugh.

I suppose you can say that I came to terms with Daisy. Realizing that I could never change her and knowing that there soon had to be an end to it, I decided to tolerate her as best I could. She was always an embarrassment. She invested in a nurses' fob watch, which dangled from the middle of the bib of her apron. It was an unnecessary expense as far as I was concerned, for I saw to it that she never used it. To her, I suppose, it was an insignia of her importance, just as the nurses' bag was a status symbol. I was never able to get accustomed to her 'oopsy daisies', and flinched every time she used the expression. There came the awful day, when we were lifting a patient, that I found myself using it; I nearly bit my tongue off.

I was treated to a detailed history of her husband's fatal disease, leukaemia, delivered as if it was something I was completely ignorant of. I couldn't resist interrupting her from time to time, when she tried to blind me with science, using words like petechia. 'Oh you mean those patches of discoloration, which appear on the skin during the advanced stages, due to the effusion of blood from damaged vessels in the periphery.' Such expressions delivered quickly did tend to take the wind out of her sails; temporarily, at any rate.

She had one habit which I could not tolerate: she criticized both Chrissie Brooks and Diane Metcalf to me, in the most insidious way, by praising my work and disparaging theirs. Eventually I told her that she was guilty of the most unprofessional behaviour, and if it didn't stop I would have to report her to Mrs Mac. She took it badly, and sulked for the rest of the day. She tried to get her own back. I noticed that both Chrissie and Diane had suddenly become distant, if not unfriendly, in their attitudes towards me. In the past we had had a deal of fun, comparing notes on Daisy's behaviour. This had now stopped and they seemed to be avoiding me. One lunch time, seeing the two together I went up to them, and as an opening gambit asked if either of them had been able to find out what Daisy's previous experience had been. Diane brusquely answered, 'Yes, I have. She began by handling dead bodies. She was the layer out for Pargetters [a Burrowdale undertaker], then she worked at Northerly as an attendent when it was a Poor Law institute, then she got married. And while we're talking about her, what's this you've been saying about Chrissie and me not teaching her enough when she was with us?' It didn't take me long to put matters right. We saw now that we were dealing with a very dangerous woman and that if we weren't careful she could destroy the spirit of comradeship, which was so much part of our working lives. We decided however not to take any immediate action.

Her next attachment was to 'Busty'. 'Why spoil the fun?' was our unanimous verdict.

Someone must have warned Daisy about 'Busty'. For the first few days she was as good as gold; indeed 'Busty' commented, 'I don't know what all the fuss is about, she seems all right to me.' Unfortunately for Daisy she couldn't restrain herself for long. She was living in the area where most of 'Busty's' patients were, and she gossiped to them about what she thought were 'Busty's' inadequacies. This was a mistake, because although the patients were aware of 'Busty's' idiosyncrasies, they loved her dearly, indeed often because of them. She was asked to have 'private words' after a number of visits, when Daisy's criticisms were repeated to her. Predictably she exploded all over the unfortunate Mrs May, but since by now Daisy had no sympathetic ears among the nurses, she had to grin and bear it. Give her credit, she again bounced up like a cork. 'Busty', though, was waiting her moment, and it fell into her lap.

A patient who had recently been discharged from hospital with a radical vulvectomy was included in 'Busty's' lists. A radical vulvectomy meant that a complete excision of the external female genital organs and groin glands had been made, and 'Busty's' job was to change the dressings daily. Now during Daisy's attachment to me, I had had two valveotomy patients, men who had had open heart surgery, involving the stretching of the heart valves – usually the mitral valve. She had taken great interest in these patients, and I had given her a complete rundown on their histories and the disease. Unfortunately for her she got her terminology mixed up, so that when 'Busty' announced that they were visiting a vulvectomy patient, she thought she knew all about it, and was anxious to demonstrate this knowledge.

'I've had experience with two cases,' she told 'Busty'. 'Will you let me get her ready for you?'

Now vulvectomies are rare, so 'Busty' knew that if any nurse had had a case it would have been talked about among us.

'All right,' she said, 'you go ahead, and I'll come in a couple of minutes time.'

'It was splendid,' 'Busty' gloated, as she described what followed. 'She rushed into the house with her "Cooee, it's only me, the district nurse." I gave her the time I'd promised, and when I went into the patient there she was, sitting in a chair, stripped to the waist, with Daisy May looking dumbfounded at her unmarked body. It was the moment I had been waiting for. I quietly told Daisy to put the clothes back on again, then asked the patient to remove her skirt and pants, and to lie on the bed, exposing her mutilated area. When I'd removed the dressings I thought Daisy was going to faint, she hadn't the stomach for it, and coming on top of the gaffe she'd made, she was swaying on her feet. When the dressing had been changed, she thought she was thankful to get back into the car. I soon changed her mood.

' "Mrs May," I said, "I have long realized that you didn't know your arse from your elbow, now it seems that you don't know your fanny from your tits." '

Whether there was any more to 'Busty's' story I never found out, for we lay around helpless with laughter.

I think all the nurses felt this would be the breaking point for Daisy. It wasn't, she continued to soldier on. She didn't change, she was a leopard. It was we nurses that altered in our attitudes towards her. We accepted her for what she was. I suppose we admired her guts in facing up to us. Now that she was a figure of fun, we knew she couldn't harm the special relationship we had with our patients, nor our loyalty one to another.

She remained as an auxiliary for a year, then left to become a student nurse in a Manchester hospital. But Burrowdale hadn't heard the last of her, for many years later she returned as a ward sister to the general hospital. I had cause to meet her again, when I went to visit a sick friend there. I had to go out of visiting hours, but it was recognized that members of the medical profession were allowed this privilege, because of our uncertain hours of work. When I arrived at the ward I spoke to a young nurse, and making myself known to her, asked to see the patient. She flushed up, seemed undecided what to do and eventually said she would have to ask sister. Up came Daisy. I greeted her like a friend; she ignored this and commented, 'It's highly irregular, but I will make an exception; you may see your friend for five minutes.' And five minutes it was, for at the end of that time she bustled me out of the ward with a 'Please try to keep to the normal visiting hours – it upsets the patients otherwise, you know.'

I did know. I also knew what pleasure it must have given Daisy May. She had had to wait many years, but eventually she did have the last word.

Chapter Thirteen

As I read back over the pages and thumb through my diary for another story, I realize that I have confined myself to Burrowdale, and given scant attention to its surrounding countryside, or to the people that live on it and from it. Nor have I written about the sea, or the fishermen and boatmen that I have nursed, and afterwards kept as friends. Perhaps I shall have another opportunity, for although this tale is about country folk, it concerns those from my own land; and while my other writings have been basic and factual, this case is frankly as sentimental as the song 'A Little Bit of Heaven', which I think of when I remember it.

Any Irishman, north or south of the border, is often homesick for his native land, even though he may have no wish to return to live there. Come to think of it the Irish are not special in this; it's possible we think we are because more of us have left our country over the years, and more songs have been written about it. I was lucky in having two soul-mates to turn to whenever I had bouts of nostalgia, in Doctor Jerry O'Dea and his wife Bernie.

Doctor Jerry had been born and brought up in County Cork; Bernie was from Dublin, and was now teaching English in a Burrowdale secondary modern school, with a thick Irish brogue. At any medical gathering we three would converge and reminisce about our early lives in our beloved country. Doctor Jerry was one for the girls, and they were like moths to his flame, for he was a handsome man, with dark blue eyes and a mop of thick black hair. It wasn't just his looks that drew them to him, they found his quiet lilting Irish voice hypnotic, and even the oaths, with which he punctuated his conversation, sounded like softly spoken prayers in their ears. Bernie might well have thought she had cause to be jealous, but like his other admirers, she knew that to Jerry it was just a game and that it was played by the rules, for I never heard a breath of scandal about him.

He had a nice turn of humour. I remember only a few years back when the doctors' club steward, answering the phone, had been asked to page a new casualty officer, a foreign doctor with a quaint-sounding name, and was having a deal of difficulty getting his tongue around it, when someone called from the sitting room – 'Doctor who?' Jerry came straight back, 'Oh don't tell me that bastard's here and all. We've got enough miracle workers around without him.'

The O'Deas had a particular kind of value to their colleagues, they acted as a sort of employment agency; Jerry could always be relied upon to find a locum, and all the doctors' resident maids were supplied by one or other of them.

It was through Doctor Jerry that I found my 'little bit of heaven' in the village of Bardale, some seven miles out of Burrowdale, up towards the hills. Bardale doesn't really deserve to be called a village, there was no church, pub or shop. It was a cluster of cottages which housed the workers of about eight neighbouring farms, a pretty enough place in the summer, but filthy in the winter when the tractors took the mud from the yards and the fields on to the road, turning it into a quagmire, so that even the slightest fall of snow or touch of frost could make driving most hazardous. Many's the time I've had to leave my car half a mile away and trudge the rest of the journey on foot. It's the kind of thing that takes the charm from the countryside. Yet when the spring came and I looked across the bay, it was possible to imagine I was once again back on the coast of Ireland, looking over Belfast from the surrounding hills. It was the view that had attracted Margaret and Peter O'Driscoll forty years before, and tempted them to buy an old caravan, having persuaded a genial farmer to let them put it in his orchard, in return for occasional labouring and household duties. Peter had thought it worth while to walk four miles every morning to catch a bus to the shipyards where he worked, and stumble back after an eight hour shift.

My patient at Bardale was Margaret, now seventy years old, and suffering from osteoarthritis as a result of an earlier injury to her hip. She'd learned to live with it, but Jerry O'Dea thought she should be given a bed bath each week and have a professional eye passed over her to make sure she was kept as comfortable as possible.

The caravan, though rickety-looking from the outside, was warm and cosy inside. It was divided into living and sleeping quarters and at a pinch three people could sit round the iron stove, with its chimney pipe leading through the roof, which on windy days would send the smoke and soot back into the caravan. Margaret couldn't bring herself to blame the weather, 'It's this terrible foreign coal, it would niver happen with a peat fire, that it wouldn't.' When the water supply had been brought into the village, the O'Driscolls had had a tap fitted inside, which dripped monotonously into an enamel basin. It was another cause for resentment, 'We're forced to pay the British government seven shillin's a year for it, it can't be roight, you know.'

Although Peter O'Driscoll had changed a little as a result of his surroundings, and the company he kept at work, Margaret had remained untouched. She refused to alter her Irish peasant ways. They fed on Irish stew, bacon ribs, boiled bacon and cabbage, and of course potatoes, always cooked in their jackets. Friday was fish day, and shopping was done from the mobile shop which called there twice a week. If ever it failed to make the hill, the farmer's wife would help her out with food; in any case there were always 'tatters'.

That Margaret was deeply religious was immediately apparent from the pictures, crucifixes and statues of the Holy Virgin that decorated the caravan. I was therefore somewhat surprised at the cold reception I received when I first visited her. I suppose I'd assumed that Doctor Jerry would have prepared the ground for me. He hadn't, for from the moment that I introduced myself it was obvious from her expression that she recognized my Ulster accent. I'm sure she would have barred the door to me if it hadn't been for the lovely Doctor O'Dea that had sent me. I tried to ingratiate myself by saying that as we were both Irish, we should get on fine together. It made matters worse, 'The black Nort is no part of Ireland at all,' she exclaimed rudely, 'And woi are you here?' she demanded. I explained that I had come to give her a bed bath. 'Oi don't need no bart, and it's niver roight that I should have to expose moi body to a stranger,' and the way she pronounced the word 'stranger' left me in no doubt but that I was an enemy from Ulster. I decided to adopt my professional manner, and eventually was able to do what I'd come to do. I did think that the respectful and reverent way in which I removed and replaced her rosary, scapular and chain of religious medallions might not have gone unnoticed, but there were no fond farewells from her when I left with my cheery 'Look forward to seeing you next week.'

So for the next few weeks it went on, and indeed would have continued to go on, had not the Catholic priest arrived one day, just as I was about to leave. 'Hallo, Patricia, fancy finding you here,' he said, then, turning to an astonished Margaret, told her how lucky she was to have an Irish Catholic nurse to look after her. She was completely shattered. She looked first at me, then at the priest, 'Oi didn't know they had Catolics in the Nort; woi didn't you tell me, me choild. Glory be to God, Fadder, is she really a Catolic?' He nodded. 'Oi should have known it from the way she's been treatin' me,' then her Irish blarney taking over, she went on, 'She's an angel of mercy, Fadder, that's what she is, she's even cut me toe-nails.'

I went away that afternoon with the feeling that my nurses' hat had been transformed into a glistening halo, and on my next visit when I told her I had been to school at the Dominican Convent in Belfast, she hugged me so tightly I feared for my ribs, though I felt my halo shining brighter than ever.

So began a relationship which I shall cherish all my life. It had a depth which is impossible for me to put into words, indeed I find it hard to understand. It had no reason or form. It was based on the unity of religion, love of a country, and love of each other. After an hour with Margaret I left refreshed and with a feeling of well being, and a zest for life. The spiritual release she gave me was beyond anything I had ever had from a priest at the confessional. I shared my life with her, and it seemed to grow from the sharing. She reasoned my doubts away and gave me a greater sense of purpose. All this I got from an old Irish peasant woman who had had little contact with the outside world for forty years.

A year after my first visit, her Peter died suddenly from a coronary thrombosis. Although he and I had been on friendly terms, I hadn't got to know him well, for he made himself scarce when I arrived, though he was always there to say good-bye when I left, and to thank me for the help he said I was giving to Margaret. I knew that his death must be a terrible blow for her, yet when I called to give what comfort I could, she behaved stoically, 'Well, Pat, it's God's holy will to be sure, and He and his Holy Mother have given us fifty years of happiness. It's for me to give tanks to them for all those beautiful years.'

Now that she was alone I was more concerned about her welfare, especially I worried about the large paraffin lamp, and what could happen should she lift it and then stumble. I could imagine the whole wooden structure which was her home becoming a blazing inferno. She also had a candle by her bedside when she read her prayers, another potential danger. I told her of my worries. 'Ah, Pat, sure your faith isn't strong enough. God and his Holy Mother are with me all the time, they would niver let me be burned.' It was then that I wished her faith was not quite so strong.

Gradually I found myself spending more and more of my off-duty time with Margaret. In the end I had to admit that I needed her more than she needed me. Our relationship lasted four years. Then one cold January morning, I had a phone call from Burrowdale hospital, telling me that a Mrs O'Driscoll had been admitted, and had given my name as next of kin. I quickly made my way there, to be told how the postman had called that morning and had found her lying unconscious on the floor of the caravan. Instead of being burned, as I had feared, Margaret had collapsed and had been nearly frozen to death. She'd been rushed to hospital and was awaiting an operation to relieve an intestinal obstruction.

When I went into the ward, I had difficulty in recognizing her, the hospital staff had transformed her, getting her clean and white, with her hitherto untidy hair braided around her head, and swathing her in a cotton nightdress. She looked so out of place, surrounded as she was by other patients. She progressed well after the operation, but it was obvious that the noise and chatter of the ward disturbed her greatly. When I told the sister that for so many years she had lived the life of a recluse, she was understanding, and Margaret was given a side ward all on her own.

Whether she decided that the time had come when she wanted to meet her maker, or whether the shock of exposure and the operation had proved too much for her, I shall never know. But after five weeks Margaret's condition began to deteriorate, and as her postman, who was a regular visitor, put it, it was obvious she was not 'going to make it'. As the end became imminent, I sat with her, holding her hand. She told me she had received the last sacraments and was now happy and contented. Her last words to me were, 'You remember, Pat, how I told you not to worry over the lamp and the candle because God and his Holy Mother were lookin' after me? I was roight, you know; they did, and they brought me to this nice clean place to die. So just you remember, me darlin', pray hard and no harm will come to you.' Then she drifted into her last sleep.

Although a very precious friend had died, my feeling of loss was not strong. Margaret's spirit has always remained with me. She, I think, gives the lie to the saying that the evil men do lives after them but the good is often buried with them.